Girl Stop, Don't Do It!

A Girl's Guide to Self-Love and Dating Relationships.

Mia Speight

This book is written in loving Memory of Mary F. Speight, my mother. She was the first to teach me how to read, starting with the King James Bible at 5 years old and who mentored me in ways that she will never know. She was a virtuous woman who served as a faithful wife, mother and Evangelist until her passing on February 8th 2025. This book is a celebration of her and the investments of knowledge, wisdom and strength she deposited into my life as her daughter and last born. Thanks Mommy, for being the light to push me to keep my promises to myself and to God.

Contents

Chapter 1

In The Beginning, God Created Standards

This is the day and age we, as women, must be very shrewd about love, dating, and relationships. If you are a woman whose intention is not to settle for second best, not end up in a miserable relationship, and eventually a marriage that ends in divorce, we must start well in order to end well. God has given us all free will to choose what we deem best for us in all aspects of life, while leaving us with all too obvious hints and cheat sheets (his word and other's experiences) to give us an inside edge. That said, the thing that affects our hearts, minds, and emotions more than anything else is relationships, especially dating relationships. Have you decided that you want to discontinue your life journey as a single person who is not in a relationship?

Are you looking to begin dating in hopes of courtship? Is this the point in your life where you feel like sharing your experiences with someone who can enrich your life and vice versa? Well, look no further.

This guide will help you sort out the old habits and attitudes that are hindering you in developing a great relationship. Some things are best left to others to experience for you, so you can learn from their mistakes. Experience is not always the best teacher. So, I am giving you advice based on my own life trials and those of others to prevent you from wasting your time and, most importantly, from the emotional heartache of relationships that are clearly not for you. My parents were married for 52 years before my mom passed away, so I was able to glean lessons from both my mother and father by over 4 decades of observation, along with my dating experiences.

When was the last time you thought about who you are and your own worth? Have you intentionally written down the qualities that make YOU unique? "You are fearfully and wonderfully made." When you know your worth, you will realize that sharing your life with any ole body just won't do. That's why it's extremely important to know what you bring to the table of any relationship, emotionally, physically, spiritually, and even financially. Remove any blinders that make your selection any less than your ideal. Don't get caught up in the world's less-than-ideal model, just to "have a man". This means that you continue to date the stereotypical suspects that have brought you little to no success in the first place. When I say ideal, I mean the person who is your spiritual equal, who balances you emotionally (If you are high-strung, he is calmer) and physically, you are capable of being attracted. These are keys to a lasting relationship that develops into courtship and eventually marriage. If you don't have basic compatibility, it will be very hard to be interested in the other qualifications listed previously. And the finances, the thing that often becomes taboo to talk about. However, if the two of you are at opposite ends of the spectrum in how you relate to money, saving, and spending, this could pose a problem. If the person is unemployed for long periods beyond their formative years, it could be a deal-breaker. Girl stop, don't do it!

You may be saying, "What does this have to do with standards?" Plenty. If you know how valuable a person you are, you will only be a boon to someone else's existence. Seems like a no-brainer, right? Well, have you ever written down your positive attributes? If not, get crackin'. Let me guess what you have done. You have written a list of the qualities you want in a potential mate. Am I right? Well, if you haven't, you also need to get crackin'. Never mind what you have heard or read from others about "the list". A person who doesn't know what they want is typically confused, and when the opportunity presents itself, they typically don't make good choices. Narrow your field. Have you ever gone to college and majored in everything? NO. You had a focus.

Back to standards now. Why do we tend to lower them when we are unsuccessful? The reason is because of the theory of low-hanging fruit. If you want easy success, you typically go for the easy victory. You get trapped in a relationship where the person adores you and is everything you want, except for the spiritual connection (meaning you both pray to God, study the scriptures regularly, and follow his word). Physically, you cringe when you have to hug; emotionally, he is on the level. Your inner thoughts tend to say, if I could just be attracted to him, this could work or maybe you are attracted, but none of the other qualities are present. Then... you are lowering your standards.

If there were no need for these pesky quality-control assurances, God would not have created them. We wouldn't have strainers to keep bitter seeds out of our refreshing lemonade drinks. There would be no background checks for job qualifications. Banks would hand out loans to everyone who walked in, like they do those free Dum-Dum lol-lipops. Get the point? We must be selective in order to limit our emotional footprint. The more times we share our intimate secrets, love, admiration, longings, and dreams with those who are not designed to handle us properly, the more damage control you must complete once God places "the one" in front of you, with whom you will ultimately spend the rest of your life. God wants us to be choosy, just don't go to the ultimate extreme and end up alone...that's not the goal. A good rule of thumb is to let the man pursue you. Initial contact to let him know you are interested is fine. After the initiation, please drop the baton. If he doesn't pick it up, the race is over. Don't reinvent the wheel. Men are created to be hunters; when you disturb this delicate balance, you keep pursuing in every aspect of the relationship. Trust me. Leaders will always lead, and followers tend to follow.

Chapter 2
Be Mindful of Developing Patterns

Ever been on a road trip and traveled across various bridges? If so, and you happened *not* to be in the driver's seat, you must have looked out on the water, seeing the rows of ripples, seemingly all fashioned in a repeating pattern. Or you might have heard the synchronized ba-bump, ba-bump, ba-bump as the car crossed the seals on the bridge or the asphalt. You recognized a pattern, and in this case, this was just to help you enjoy the subtle nuances, the beauty of being out and about on a road trip. Don't lose that curiosity or perceptive sense. Many times —when meeting someone —depending on your personality type, you may be the "all or nothing" type, the "play it cautious, you've been hurt before type", or the "just take life as it comes and don't force anything" type. Whatever your type, it is important to know how the person you may be interested in may respond. Let's take my type, for example. I am the "all or nothing" type, so my tendency is to be a loyal friend that you can call on for anything, anytime. My type is very demonstrative, with my friends and even more so in romantic relationships. This means that if you need help, I will gladly put my plans aside to put you first (wink- most of the time, not all the time). Perhaps you want breakfast? I will gladly cook it for you, and depending on how much I like you, I may bring it to you. You need money here, take it and don't think about returning it (If I have it, it's yours, if I don't, sorry fah yah). And as the famous line from the musical group SKYY in 1981, "If you need someone to talk to, call me." The whole sentiment is that you can be a person who gives of themselves quite regularly, BUT, and this is a BIG BUT. If the other person you are interested in seems all too frequently unavailable, a pattern has formed. You call to see if this person needs help with something you both have planned, and the phone is answered immediately. The lines of communication are open, whether it's a text to let you know they are on the way, a call to ask if you need anything, or maybe a simple good morning message. BUT, as soon as the help is received or you give them what they need, you get the voicemail or the text you sent them returned at 1am, when you are sleeping.

Needless to say, no one likes exerting effort for naught, or for the affections of someone who is emotionally un-available. It really doesn't matter if you take your time, do it gradually, or do it quickly, as long as you're open to the possibilities of getting to know someone. If the patterns of non-communication, forced dialogue, conditional communication based on someone needing something from you, and constant unavailability, are patterns that by no means will get you to the healthy relationship you desire. Even though it may be tempting for the go-getter-type such as myself, to take the reins and dive full speed ahead, thinking, "I'll just get the ball rolling, and he will take from there." WRONG! See the patterns and quickly make a mental note to yourself that you are worth more and have a lot to offer someone who is willing to invest time and attention at the same level you are. Keep rolling along the highway of life, ba-bump, ba-bump, ba-bump.

Chapter 3
You Can't Run From You

Knowing the appropriate time and place in your life to begin, develop, and desire a relationship is not always easy to forecast. The bible speaks of the appropriate timing in Ecclesiastes 3 and more specifically the relational type in verse 5b portion, "a time to embrace, and a time to refrain from embracing;" Its often times when we are at a point in our lives when we feel tired of being lonely, not everything is working out according to our master plan, or all is well but we haven't quite learned or healed internally from all the relationship follies of our past is when we go forging full speed ahead to find a companion. Yes, no one is perfect; however, there is a time when cultivating a friendship/relationship is ideal. The key is that you can't use the comfort of being in another created world with someone else as an escape. There are plenty of things we do in life to avoid the obvious work that must be done at home, on OURSELVES. A few illustrations should help you get a clearer picture of what I mean. You're at home, and you don't feel like putting the work into preparing food for yourself to eat. You have all the materials that you need to make a meal, pots and pans, utensils, oils, meats, and vegetables. What's the one thing that you lack? The discipline to make what would most often be a healthier meal at home. By reading a recipe, hashing out the details of the proper amounts of ingredients, cutting, prepping, and pre-heating the oven. Waiting for the meal to cook at the right temperature, then finally being able to nourish yourself with the fruits, well, in this case, the foods of your labor. Instead of doing the previous, you disregard the money, time, and effort it took to shop for food. You leave all the groceries that you've spent your hard-earned dollars to buy in the refrigerator. Out you go, to purchase fast food, order online, or maybe a carry-out platter to cure your appetite. Once you receive your delicacies prepared by others, you realize they're too greasy, too salty, and overpriced. You come home, and the next day you face that exact same situation. The solution given was only temporary. You must learn to discipline yourself to prepare healthier foods at home.

Another illustration. You are in the quiet house alone; it's too quiet. You try to avoid your own thoughts, you avoid being meditative, or reading to build up your mental capacity. Solution: you try to turn on music, or you indulge in binge-watching your favorite shows for hours on end. Maybe you inundate yourself with booking every weekend to go out with friends... taking photos to post on social media, giving all your followers a false sense that you have a perfect life. At the beginning of the year, you've promised yourself that you were going to be more conscientious about your spiritual life, working on any negative personality traits that show up in your relationships, or changing the negative script that keeps rolling in your mind consistently. What did you learn? No matter what you do to avoid your inner self~ the complexities, hang-ups, traits that you (and others who dated you) find unappealing, you cannot. Once you execute all your plans, make detours from doing the work that ultimately makes you a better person. You arrive right back in the same place...right back with *yourself*. There is a reason that we have to love ourselves first, not so we can be ego maniacs. No! So we can properly love others. The two greatest commandments in the word of God we find in Matthew 22:37-40 (NIV).

37 Jesus replied: "'Love the Lord your God with all your heart and with all your soul and with all your mind.'**38** This is the first and greatest commandment. **39** And the second is like it: 'Love your neighbor as yourself.'**40** All the Law and the Prophets hang on these two commandments." (NIV)

If you know that there are places in your life that need improvement: being a better cook, learning to control negative thoughts, having a better attitude, and growing in your spiritual life by reading the Bible and attending a bible study with a fellowship of believers. Whatever the case may be. You can't run from yourself. No matter what you do, that same you will keep showing up, you will notice in your interactions with others that you haven't done the work on yourself that is required. Striving toward a goal and outlining the work that's required has its way of eliminating some negative traits, no matter how minuscule. Will you be perfect? Probably not. However, you will feel more comfortable with yourself, and so will whoever you enter into a relationship with.

Create an action plan to start every morning with a routine that fosters positive thinking and self-actualization. **I CAN** make better choices in relationships. **I AM** worthy of *REAL* love. I will **NOT** reduce myself to an abusive relationship, just to avoid being alone. **I WILL** achieve my career goals. **It IS** possible to have a life that is pleasing and positively affects others. **I AM** an asset. **I AM** the prize in the relationship.

There is one thing you cannot deny: the one factor in all the past failed relationships was YOU. YOU have to make better choices to mitigate the damage to your spirit. YOU are the only one who can change your thinking and unwise choices. You can run from everyone else, but you can't run from you.

Chapter 4

Are You Fit For A Relationship?

You wake up, go to the bathroom, shower, and get ready for your day. After you are already awake, you still feel tired and sluggish as if you stayed out all night, but you didn't; it's a weeknight. You look in the mirror and say, "I am really tired of having this belly fat" or "I really want to start going to the gym to get in better shape". You scurry off to find clothing that flatters your figure and also makes you feel good, professional, and attractive. Only to find yourself running late because it seems as if nothing fits the way you'd like or think it should. "Does this look silly together?" you ask yourself, because these are the only items that fit well, but may not match up as you'd like.

You finally get to work, or your meeting, and you feel like you have already clocked in major hours just getting yourself clothed and in your right mind. Body image autonomy is seemingly further from the grasp of most women these days. We are conflicted by tons of media ads, billboards, YouTube videos, Instagram pages, television, and commercials that scream at us that we need to be more beautiful than ever before. Buy this style of hair care products, use this type of lipstick, get these lashes, and go get this type of nail treatment. We become all too distracted by the decorations of the exterior that we forget that fitness and health are more important than anything that can be removed by fingernail polish remover, the dry cleaners, or the trash can. Our body is our temple, we must never forget to give it the utmost care it needs to be fit…not according to everyone else's standards, but according to the goal you have set in your mind for YOU.

Now is the time to tell yourself, "I will keep my promise to myself." No New Year's resolution this time. It's pertinent in any relationship that you have a healthy body image. Fitness and proper nutrition are, and always have been, the *weapons of mass destruction* to demolish bad health and put you on track to building your body up with the right fuel to power your life.

The goal of being fit, can and should be an internal motivation first; however, it does not exclude you from receiving external motivation from a friend or a new relationship. Regardless of the reason, it's wise to start your journey to become the best you can be. You will have to prepare for opposition, as well as for those who wish you well in your fitness endeavors. There have been instances of people experiencing major pushback from their family, especially during family gatherings. A young lady started out on her fitness journey, and her immediate family has had a history of poor health (diabetes, high blood pressure, obesity, gate problems, high cholesterol, etc.) along with mental health problems. She vowed to start being in better control of what she ate, even at family functions, so she would stop the guilty feeling associated with binge eating that is all too commonplace with these affairs. So she planned to bring items she enjoyed eating to grill at the cookout. She brought salmon because she was trying to avoid red meat and other poultry, which she thought would not work well with her body. In the past, when she came to family functions, she was normally ridiculed for refusing food items offered to her because they often did not make her feel well after consumption, or sometimes she would not eat at all. So this time around, she thought things would be different because they would be willing to grill her fish with no big deal. The ridicule persisted, with insults being flung to the likes of "Oh, you think that you are better than everyone else?", or "You have to have 'Special' food in order for you to hang out with us," and on and on. It will take a strong will to succeed, to stand up against these attacks on your well-being. Please understand it's not your responsibility to make people understand or to get permission to change your life. Forge ahead in a way that lets them know we can still be family, without compromising my health.

Please know that being fit is something that's not only physical but also mental. This info is reinforced by over 53 peer-reviewed articles. Mental wellness is an offspring of physical wellness; if you tend to have poor health, it can lead to increased psychological issues within, and in external relationships. Please don't ask yourself whether you are perfect in this area; instead, ask whether this is a goal, you intend to follow through on, whether you are in a relationship or not. Are you fit for a relationship with yourself?

When was the last time you dedicated the same time and attention you invest in your hair and nails to the gym or healthy meal prep? There are 168 hours in the week; you can implement that goal by joining an inexpensive gym and starting to go 2 to 3 times a week for 30 minutes as an act of self-love. There is also the option of walking in the park a few days a week and using the outdoor fitness equipment provided by most parks if you are not a big fan of the gym. When you are taking care of your physical self, such as regular self-check-ups and visits to the doctor, monitoring your weight, maintaining good dental hygiene, maintaining a cardio regimen, and learning to properly lift weights to keep your body firm. You are, in fact, becoming fit for a loving relationship with yourself and will be better prepared for the relationship you desire with another.

As a retired personal trainer with over 15 years of industry experience. I became a haphazard counselor of sorts as well. It became part of my job to listen to a person's issues and how they related to why they struggled to achieve their goals. This was double-sided because, at times, I trained the husband and wife separately, and I became privy to the deeper issues that plagued the relationship as an offshoot of being unhealthy. Ills impacting the intimacy of the marriage, including erectile dysfunction, the woman feeling unattractive, low libido, the husband losing attraction, fibroids, inflammation, and feeling extreme exhaustion. As singles, we have a good amount of time to prepare physically to get ahead of these problems, but all too frequently, we focus on fast-forwarding our single stage of development. In most of these cases, neither spouse wanted to offend the other by having the hard conversations about fitness and making health a priority. There were also times when one spouse had made the commitment to change their life for the better, while the other was resistant or a saboteur of the other's progress. Please consider if you are recreationally compatible with your ideal mate. It's not wise to want a man with a six-pack if you hate exercising; it's typical that like attracts like-minded.

Now is the time to decide how you want your fitness and health to be or not to be. Most people you meet in life will not change too much from who they already are, especially as we get into middle age. I encourage you to make fitness a lifestyle, not a quick hack to look good just for a summer or vacation. It's possible!

Chapter 5
Social Media: Follow or Not?

A s Shakespeare similarly put it. To follow or not to follow, that is the question? Although Hamlet's dilemma was a much greater fight, to go to battle or to kill him self....really ours is not that serious, is it? In this social media-driven culture, relevance, importance, and self-worth seemed to be misconstrued, twisted, if you will, into this web-based conundrum we call the World Wide Web. We were introduced to Facebook in 2004, and since then, it has given birth to all things social media, like Instagram, Tik Tok, WhatsApp, and Snapchat. People use these outlets at any given time of the day to escape work, to be informed on street culture, be in the know of what's trending, discover the latest memes, sports clips, booty pics, post pictures of family and friends, slide into DMs, watch entertaining dance clips, and post selfies, post selfies, and post selfies again. To some, this phenomenon has blown right over top of their heads, and they go on living life through the old-fashioned way of calling, perhaps texting, and meeting people the organic way of just living life up close and in person.

However, when it comes to dating and relationships, things are *not* as easy. Say you happened to be on social media when you met another person who is on social media as well. You start by following them and liking their pictures. Is this what is best or ideal? Dating becomes serious, and now you're in a relationship. As you become one another's biggest fans by liking and following, you notice that neither of you comments on the other's pics. Is this a protective safety net for the relationship to blossom, devoid of random extras interfering? Or is this a ploy to seem readily available, for either person to be seen as single? Are you monitoring your new love interests' page? Are you looking at who and what they are taking pictures with when they are not with you? Is it driving you a bit stir-crazy to see the same females commenting and he responding as if they have a closer relationship than you do? Chances are, you don't need to follow them so closely until you are sure your relationship itself is *real* and intact.

Social media has now become the newest, most effective devastator of relationships, as this was never an issue in years past, when all potential suitors were safely tucked in other states or countries, for that matter. Your man or potential man could not scroll to see semi-nude beach pics of someone who sparks his interest and simply DM for their attention, which might very well be reciprocated. Girl stop, don't do it! Please focus on the red flags you might be missing while you are so busy liking a gang of selfies or pics he takes with "friends". Ask a ton of questions about how important social media is in their everyday life. Can you go on a date with him, without him checking his phone constantly? Can you have a stimulating conversation about his life goals and the latest book he is reading? If he is reading at all. Don't be duped by the looks of what appears to be a perfect life they portray on social media; see if they have substance and are not so self-consumed that the best treatment you receive is a heart or thumbs up on your social media page. See if what is presented is true. Ask about the friends in the pictures. If possible, try to talk to those friends to see what kind of person you are dealing with. Try to arrange a time when all of you can go out, so you are certain that the individual you are dating is *not* operating as a single person **or** in another relationship when you are not around. It's too easy to live a double life on social media because each person controls how they are perceived. Social media plays a crucial role in most individuals' lives, helping them connect in healthy ways; however, you want to be aware if it's an obsession or a ploy to collect various women for the bait-and-switch. Ask the person you are dating, "Who am I Dating?" "What is the first thing you do in the morning?" Are they praying, are they reading the paper, checking the news, or checking their news feed on social pages? All things must be balanced, and some people must use this system to promote work or job opportunities; the majority of creatives use it as a tool. However, if you have a 9-to-5 and spend most of your time on these platforms, it may be used to hunt for other women (or men), creating an unhealthy habit of not developing good conversation or character.

Don't get caught up in competition on social media in your relationships. You might say to yourself, "Why would I do that? You can do it without even realizing it. If you are dating a person who is a user, an attention seeker, or is running through women, so to speak. They have no real interest in you and will sometimes friend and follow you, purposely waiting until you post so they can post right after; they are bent on stealing your thunder. It's a very unhealthy game to feed into the adoration they seek, keeping them feeling good about themselves while at the same time making you feel less important to them. Am I saying this is for everyone? By no means. However, there are clear signs of attention seeking in certain personality disorders that allow men to manipulate women. Read their header. If a person says they are a personal trainer as a profession and you never hear them talking about training clients, what are they doing if not lying to promote a certain image? Ask them what certification they received to train people, and what type of insurance they are enrolled in to protect themselves and the client in the event of an injury. Competition is not always about posting at the same time. Competition can also be as subtle as a person trying to seem more intelligent than others, or to be selected based on what you think of the image they present on social media. Questions are key to using your intellect, not your emotions, when deciding whether to meet random people we cannot verify.

Pay attention to *consistency*, it's easy for him to send messages saying how pretty you are and have a wonderful day *IN THE BEGINNING*. However, you must take special note that if the compliments slow down and you find yourself taking over, or he gets angry that you haven't responded within the time frame or in the manner he wants, this poses a problem. Ladies, we must be aware that, like no other time before, the internet and social media are a virtual hook-up buffet where you can place multiple fishing poles in the water and wait for something to bite. In some cases, people just cast a net and chum in large quantities. Hopefully, if you are reading this book, you are *not* interested in someone for "One night only," like the Jennifer Hudson song; you want something forever and are tired of being treated as an object rather than a human being. Let's use our intellect in the social media sphere.

And NOW LADIES (And gentlemen who may be reading to strengthen their game)! The OH so talked about DM, or direct message, (for the social media unsavvy). This has been the talk of posts on some popular pages that promote healthy relationships, people meeting, finding their partner in life, and marrying their best friend. Some give their testimonies of how they first met their spouse after sending DMs to their crush or someone they were interested in. Now, let me give you my personal testimony of how I learned the hard way that not all DM's are good DM's.

A gentleman, and I use that term loosely, began to send me private messages, love bombing so to speak, lots of compliments, and caring gestures. I ignored it for a time. Then, after a while, I looked at his page, and it was inconsistent; some pictures were between 6 and 8 years old. Not just a couple for throwback Thursday or Flashback Friday, no, I'm talking about 45% of the profile, and the other half looked like his older, heavier set brother. So I'm asking myself, "How old is this person?" I like the younger version, but ladies, I need you to read these words very carefully...I DID NOT use my *intelligence*. I *overlooked* this obviously double-sided person, who seemed to want so badly to relive their younger "hay days" and give them a chance.

I allowed their messages. This means, for the (off the social media grid folks), on IG (Instagram), if you want to have a conversation with a stranger you haven't followed, you must press a button to allow them to have a conversational exchange. If you do not allow their messages, you can press decline or just let them sit there with no response from you. Anyhow, after allowing this person, he proceeded with all the niceties, "Good morning, Sunshine" with 7 emojis following, flowers, smiles, and likes. Every day, sometimes 3 or 4 times. At this time in my life, I was very busy, working on projects and being cast as an actress, almost every other day. So when I didn't respond the way they wanted, they got pushy (another sign, ladies: run like the wind). I once again did not use my GOD given intelligence and overlooked it as eager doting. After more and more pushes, messages, and finally a selfie, he sent. I noticed in the selfie that he looked older than many of the pics in his profile because he let his beard grow out. Clean shaven he did look a little younger. I was around my family at the time and showed them the picture. They immediately said, "He is too old!" I refer the message from my family back to him, perhaps to brush him off in my mind. Once again, I did not use my judgment and proceeded anyway. Later, we planned to meet offline.

Once I met him, I got a kinda sick feeling like something was off, like he wasn't into women at all or *something*, my gut was saying Nah Brah, but my emotions said oh, give him a chance, you've been single for soooo long. Fast forward, and it seemed he was pushing me into a relationship at break neck speed. Ladies, let's slow down and digest this. A man is looking to start a "committed relationship" at break neck speed. Sidebar bar, the only other time in my life this happened was when I was on a dating site, and this was a strategy, I caught onto that guys use to get your cookies. Because now, after knowing you as a person for a good five minutes at best, they know enough about you to commit? YEAH Right! Ladies, this is no prize. If your goal is marriage, not girlfriend, please STOP, STOP, and ask yourself, "Is this how this works?" (Maybe for him to get what he wants, but not for you). DON'T DO IT!

Did I pull back a bit at this point? Yes, somewhat, but not enough to use my intellect and sans emotion. I thought about it after a couple of dates and then agreed (hey, we all make mistakes, and that is what makes us hopefully

LEARN). He told me he was dating with a purpose, he wanted to be married and have a kid. I fell for the exterior presented (beware of appearances) and for words without qualified actions: a single man, well-dressed to a fault, above middle age, with no kids, a nice home, a nice vehicle, and a good job. We as ladies tend to fast-forward in our minds -- to put ourselves into the marriage picture and say to ourselves, "all he needs is me to make a nice, cohesive relationship." A couple of weeks to months go by, and the honeymoon phase quickly dies off: under-the-breath potshots, no phone calls from him when I travel for work for several days, slow or no responses to text messages. No deep conversations, no intellectual stimulation of any kind unless it was initiated by me. All the doting faded, and I found myself alone most every weekend, pursuing his attention, time, and the fulfillment of the things promised in the relationship. Watching him closely after kissing goodbye, I could see his disdain for me as he walked away. A cruel spirit lurked behind the eyes of that man with the polished look so meticulously put together, so interested in me in the beginning. We were always on the verge of breaking up or broke up in such a short time frame. And then the epiphany comes to me. I ignored all the signs and dove headlong into a fake relationship. Later confirmed by himself, from his own lips, just a few weeks before the relationship was over, he stated he was a narcissist.

This was well before the term was popularized all over the internet. Keep in mind, this was almost 9 or 10 years ago.

It hit me, "Do you even know what that really means?" I asked myself. I did some spotty research, but again wanted to show the love of God to someone who just probably had a tough childhood and could be loved out of this bad behavior, NOT! After months of wasted time, this person was honest enough to say he didn't want kids and didn't want marriage to me (my spirit said he didn't want it with anyone, for that matter). I fled the relationship immediately and then read for hours about narcissists. I became angry that I overlooked all the gut feelings, red flags to indicate the signs of a person reeling you in to destroy you, and to use you for their ego boost, and discard you. This person said and did everything they needed to, inconsistently, to reap the benefits of a person who genuinely loves too fast, but he did not return those sentiments. They are heartless, literally miserable individuals. All from a DM. Are all DM's bad? No. But you have to understand that the nature of social media allows people to study you, your page, your videos, and your thoughts. If you put too much of your inner feelings on the internet for all the world to see, especially on a public page. BEWARE and stop, don't jump into something or fall for someone so fast that you keep disregarding the inconsistencies of what they say versus what they do. If this is happening now, RUN! If it has already happened, forgive yourself and the person, and LEARN not to make the same bad choices that lead to mistakes without properly vetting potential mates. Don't be bitter, be better. Accept DM's with caution.

Chapter 6
Change Your Mindset, Stop The Cycles

And be renewed in the spirit **of your mind**.
Ephesians 4:23 (KJV)

And the peace of God, which surpasses all understanding, **will guard your hearts and minds** through Christ Jesus.
Philippians 4:7 (NKJV)

As a man or woman thinketh in the heart so is he or she (Proverbs 23:7). Whether you believe this or not, doesn't mean it's not truth. Please stop right now and sit in silence for 2-3 minutes, unguided, just let your thoughts run. Where does your mind go? What are you thinking? Negative thinking? Remembering the last person who hurt you? What someone said that hurt your feelings? What someone said at work? Are you thinking, I'm tired? Why am I overweight? Why am I still SINGLE? What am I going to do about my finances? All these thoughts are coming into your mind automatically, without you having to conjure them up. Why?? It is because we are never taught to *consistently* press the RESET buttons on our minds – to rehearse positive thinking as its substitute. To literally change any and every negative thought that comes into our minds into something that promotes a healthier, non-bitter, and brighter outlook. Yes, some of you may have heard the scripture verse from 2 Corinthians 2:5b, "take captive every thought and make it obedient to Christ Jesus"; some have never heard it, or you may not believe it's applicable to you. Whatever the case may be. What we do with our thoughts, is strongly interlinked to our outlook on life.

Have you ever evaluated the characteristics of the people you dated in the past? Is there a pattern? – Yes! Not only with the individuals you dated but with the person who did the selecting, the person inviting those individuals into your life, YOU. We, myself included, have gone through cycles of dating the same person in character, even though these were two totally different human beings. Physically, you have a type; mentally, you have a type; and spiritually, you have a type. Cycles are so tricky, because as we age, we sometimes become weaker, we bend the standards set for ourselves, and fall right back into the types of people we do not want (not just physically), but spiritually and mentally. Why? Because we keep thinking about that person from the previous relationship, you, yes YOU, let your mind wander and reminisce on a failed relationship and replay different scenarios in your head of your experience. Or perhaps now that you have learned from that experience, you may replay what you would have or could have done differently to get the upper hand so they would not have hurt you as they did. This could go on for days, weeks, and years before you realize that I have been thinking the same negative things for years, and I have not stopped myself from thinking in this way- but maybe for a couple of hours on Sunday, Sabbath, or Friday when you go to a social function. This can be applied to every thought you have; apply it to whatever you choose, whether it might be work, family, friends, an ex-spouse, an ex-relationship, your goal to get into better physical condition, etc. In your mind, you have attached a blame or shame mechanism to each failure you have experienced. You revel in it, rehearse it, you tell it to everyone who is willing to listen and even those who can't stand to hear any more of what you cram down their throats, forcing them to digest the poisonous toxins of your past repeatedly --- not for them to gain a better understanding of who you are, but to *rehash* what your mind has *not* been healed from. You have not taken the time to understand what YOU must do. You have failed to regularly focus on changing your mindset. Have you sought out counseling to deal with the issues of why your mind keeps repeating negative experiences? That might be something to look into (FYI, your mind is just as important as your manicure). Seeking professional help is not a sign of weakness; it shows that you value yourself and don't want to destroy future opportunities or relationships with old mindsets that haven't yet yielded what you seek. Do you have any history of psychological problems or mental health issues in your family that you are unaware of? If so, the cycle of not dealing with those issues stops here with you. We must continue to learn and grow to become the finished product, showing others that it can be done.

A bicycle has 2 wheels, and a chain is only attached to one of them. The rear wheel has this chain, so the rider can use muscular force to push the pedals forward, transferring the rear wheel's propulsion to the front wheel. The chain is placed over a single gear and can switch when it reaches the maximum capacity speed or when there is insufficient force from the pedal to propel it forward. Both wheels must always spin forward (in a circle), no matter how fast or slow they are; they are unified in their efforts and not divided. One wheel cannot go north while the other goes south, one wheel cannot go east while the other goes west. Why? Because the handlebars control the movement of both wheels, cycling is a repeated motion that achieves one objective: getting the rider from point A to point B. If at any time the rider of the bicycle wants to change the direction of the bike, he must continue to pedal while turning the handlebars, with both wheels going in the same direction. The only way the wheels can go in separate directions is if they are disconnected from the bike. The front is the easiest to remove because it doesn't have a chain, and newer models let you pop a thumb switch in the center of the wheel and take the wheel right off. The rear wheel, however, is more difficult to remove because you have to remove the chain and loosen the bolts that connect it to the gears. A concerted effort must be made to remove the rear wheel. The point is: In order to get out of cyclical behavior, you must make a strategic effort to remove the chain from your mindset and reverse the habit that was formed of habitually going in circles in your actions, negative thinking patterns, choices, people who stunt your intellectual, spiritual, and relational growth, and set new healthy habits to replace them.

Who is your chain attached to in the bicycle of life? Who is steering your thoughts? Who are you connected to? Do they have a toxic cycle of thinking that is spilling over into your mind? Remember, wherever one wheel goes, the other is sure to follow. It's time to take inventory first of you, then of others, who are in your inner circle of influence. Repeated thoughts are contagious.

Get your monkey wrench and remove the wheel of your life, set it on the course of an abundant life free of stereotypes, pity wallowing, depression, camping out in your past, resentment, the blame game, and being a mediocre Bob or Betty. No one will fix your life for you...not even Iyanla!

Chapter 7
Observation Is Key

I believe there is a built-in mechanism that wires us to have some love or at least appreciation for people watching. We've all done it before. You may be in the mall waiting on a loved one to finish shopping in a store you are not interested in going into, so you sit outside on those middle benches and watch the groups of people walk by. You observe their clothing, whether they are fashionable or NOT, women - if they have on make-up, a man's walk, his body frame, if he is wearing a wedding ring. A family with children is getting pizza, including cute little girls, a woman with bad posture or ill-fitting clothes, and a guy with a sneaker bag, talking loudly on the phone with his friends. A woman walking alone with a nice pair of jeans that fit her just right, the length of a man's well-maintained beard, and his broad shoulders... whoever, we like to be voyeurs and observe other people as a form of entertainment. Why oh why, pray tell do we not observe the people who have piqued our interests when it comes to dating relationships? Why have we lost this curiosity until later, when we have a sneaky suspicion that our relationship has gone awry?

I know that watching from a distance has become harder than ever before in this day and age. You may not work with the individual of interest, or have mutual friends with whom you can see them on a daily, much less weekly, basis. It does pose a bit of a challenge when you are both in two separate circles. So this action must be purposeful. I really mean it, it does. We all have cell phones, so this will be easier than you think. When you first meet someone in person, you always have a gut feeling. Do you not? Well, how many times have you jotted that gut feeling down in your phone to review it after your date? Now is the time to start! You observe something kinda off, but you ignore it, maybe an offhand comment or a saying that is continuously repeated, but you are not sure what that means, so you never ask, and you typically just brush it off as no big deal. NO more! Pull out your phone and start documenting. Don't be in a rush as a woman to go into the fantasy land of being a couple, when you are only in the dating phase, just because he looks handsome, or let the way you feel get the best of you. Be an investigative reporter for the party of one. This information is for your eyes only - to make an informed decision. Is there consistency in your treatment from the first time you interacted till now? Are there any items you notice left behind in this person's space that are not from you when you visit? What are you seeing in plain sight that this person doesn't need to communicate to you verbally, but that is as big as a billboard and can't be missed? WRITE IT DOWN. Don't get caught up in the physical attraction and forget to be in observation mode. Now, contrary to the popular slogan at airports or on major highways, "see something, say something," this is NOT what you will do. Why? Partly because you want to make your own decision about who this person is. You don't want to disrupt them being who they are on a regular basis. You don't want to alert them to your observations. It's just like the saying goes: if someone is showing you who they are, believe them the first time.

You must assess, over time, as a friend: ask yourself, "Is this what I really want?" Is this person compatible with the goals I have set? Do they have a vision that I can assist with? Do we make a good team intellectually?

Next time you watch your favorite program, be aware of every detail and nuance, even down to what the characters typically wear and how they talk/interact with other characters. Some people have perfected the art of observation so much so, that when a character does something odd, they immediately take notice and say something like, "That's not like them or They never would do that!" If we can track fictional characters' motives, moves, mannerisms, and reactions, we should be able to patiently sip our tea or coffee as we watch and wait for our interactions with people we're interested in. We can save loads of time if we have that same 20/20 hindsight while we're in observation mode.

Only time will tell. You must be patient and let time tell. On the contrary, rushing anything will make things happen unnaturally and set things off course. Observing is keeping a good enough distance that you are emotionally unattached, if you must abandon ship, so to speak. Knowing that no one is perfect is always good; yet the goal of being friends or dating is to observe, to collect data, to see if you'd like to go further. Some qualities, or the lack thereof, don't make for good friendships or even relationships. Granted, there may be times when compatibility isn't there, but the person is honest, genuine, and not looking to devalue you just to please themselves. Their motives are pure, and they insist on a platonic relationship first and foremost. For this person, there is no rush to get to know you, and really, there is no end to getting to know you. They (the person of interest) are positioning themselves as a lifelong friend, not a plaything, a deceiver, or a person looking for something (for nothing) without investing much of themselves in the process.

Keep this in mind: when you were in high school and even college, you completed some experiments using the steps of observation, question, hypothesis, experiment, analysis, and conclusion. Think back to when you did a petri dish test... that circular glass was covered with red nutrient agar, which is the best medium for growing things like bacteria/viruses. The teacher gave you a long cotton swab or a skinny metal instrument and assigned you to go out and find different surfaces to swab or collect specimens. After placing the collected specimen into the petri dish in a zig-zag pattern, you had to wait. Nothing appeared immediately; even so, you let the project sit and germinate, so to speak, and later, after you observed the dish, you could visibly see larger raised patterns. When you looked through a microscope, it magnified the species' activity or growth pattern, and you could therefore name what it was by the patterns it created. Observe, Observe, Observe.

Chapter 8
Kill The Bitter Root

If, at this time in your life, you find yourself single and with few qualified dating prospects, you are not alone. At times, you may scroll through social media and see pages dedicated to people falling in love and getting married, or posts from people traveling with their significant other; it can make it seem like everyone is in a relationship but you. At times, you can be generally happy to see others find love and fulfillment in a new relationship or marriage. But, as the Bible scriptures say, "Hope deferred makes the heart grow sick." You may start to think or even compare yourself by having a mindset that says, "What's so special about them?" or "He or she is not even that attractive." You may think you have the same or better qualities and feel that it should be your turn next, but it doesn't seem to be coming like you'd thought it would, at this particular time in your life. It's hard not to get caught up in a negative thought pattern. Especially as you see close friends who have already married and had kids distance themselves, mostly unintentionally, from their single friends because their life priorities have shifted toward a more familial setting. This is understandable for some, yet hard to navigate for others who find themselves reaching out, calling, or texting friends who are disengaged. Personally, I remember hanging out with my single friends and asking them to attend functions with me, and from that event, sharing time with them, they met their spouse. As time passed, I didn't get any phone calls or texts from the person with whom I shared my clients and inner circle. It definitely stings, to know that you may have been the catalyst for their happiness, and that once they were coupled and later married, the friendship no longer seemed important. Hurts tend to mount, and if we are not careful, we, as singles, begin to get a bit dissatisfied with the loyalty of "friends" and honestly feel that it was a friendship with an expiration date. We are not naïve to the fact that there are seasons to all things, and that some unhealthy friendships are best left at a distance or avoided altogether. However, if the friendship was a healthy one where joy and great life experiences were shared, you can almost feel the same pain you'd feel in a dating relationship that ended abruptly. This is what we must come to terms with and find healing—avoid the bitter root that would keep us from making more friends and from keeping people at arm's length.

The other scenario is the one we know of oh, too well... the relationship we thought was the one, and we put our heart and soul into it to make it work out. We felt settled, impervious to the ills of reality, yet blind to the red flags that said this wouldn't last long. Foolishly in love, we forged ahead in unconditional love, thinking the person would change. The thrill of relationship victory pales in comparison to the agony of defeat. Neither partner in the relationship wants to be the first to throw in the towel and say, "This is NOT GOING TO WORK". Being unequally yoked, or as some say, trying to fit the proverbial square peg into a round hole. The difficulties of the thoughts that can't be deleted in your mind on how you cared and what you did for that person can leave you resentful if you are not careful to purge yourself of the past. Training your mind not to keep beating yourself up for being too kind or for overlooking things that should have clearly raised concern. You feel like you've wasted an outfit, so to speak, on the relationship. All your emotions, love, attention, and finances could have been put to better use. Hindsight is always 20/20, but the sharp, excruciating discomfort of loneliness can push some to make unwise, hasty decisions driven by temporary emotions. Thinking it over, some would choose loneliness over the stress that has penetrated the mind, due to the emotional detachment process that must take place in order to be a healthy single again. The blame game comes into play, we feel like something was done to us, we were somehow forced against our will, most likely duped or deceived into a situation that once in, was not at all what we signed up for. We teeter on the thin line of bitterness and acquiescence. This too is a decision!! We can continue to play the victim, or we can take responsibility for our choices and make better ones - not rush into decisions without proper observation. Easier said than done, we all know.

So, if you are in this dry, barren land called bitterness, how do you reach the lush land of happiness and contentment? Here are some things I have tried and continue to do, to maintain a positive attitude. The goal is to emit a pleasing fragrance to a new potential suitor if your gift is not that of singlehood; furthermore, it's a good thing to be a pleasing person in general, even if you don't want a relationship. It improves friendships, interactions with colleagues, family, and casual acquaintances. Everyone wants to be around nice, friendly, good-natured people. I think that should be a goal for you and me. This is not something that is achieved overnight; it is like fitness—you must work at it daily to maintain it. First, I tried taking a negative thought, such as resentment, and changing it to a positive one, like determination. Using negative energy and turning it into positive energy to propel me forward and achieve my life's goals. Example no.1, I want to become proficient in a second language, so instead of mulling over the past or listening to the same songs on the radio. I listen to language apps to challenge my mind and improve my language skills. Example no. 2: This determination is exercised literally when I aim to focus my discipline on exercising 6 days a week and abstaining from eating after a certain hour in the evening. Again, I am using my energy to battle myself and my bad habits, my laziness, my attitude, and I, at times, totally forget about the past. This leads me to Example no. 3, I started to fulfill the promises I made to myself about reading more books, writing, getting into a deeper connection spiritually by praying and reading the bible, I completed my plan to become debt free, learning more about finances, implementing a saving strategy and going places that I've had a strong desire to go -- with or without someone to go with me. Will this totally eradicate those negative feelings? NO. But this will greatly reduce them, and when the bitterness closely related to anger arises, you can redirect. It's just like a pop-up ad on your computer; if it's something unwanted, and most times it is, we press the X button at the top right-hand corner, and it disappears. Also, like an unwanted email... we quickly scroll to the bottom, find the unsubscribe button, delete the email, and move on with life. We don't have to live in the past to reconnect to toxic relationships; we don't have to hold grudges and be bitter. We are better than that, and that person is the one who has an attractive spirit. Something that some people can't quite put a finger on, but they like it. Let the fresh new leaves of hope, self-mastery, self-love, and self-control pierce the ground...breakthrough. To attract it, we must do some gardening. Admit the bitter root exists (if it in fact does), dig it up with the spade of forgiveness and toss it out once and for good like some old torn-up granny panties, laugh, and move forward to your destiny. Smile, the future is bright!

Chapter 9

You Are Highly Valued, Single

Have you ever been to a jewelry store to look at diamonds? Weather you were on the brink of a real engagement, or a man used this mind game to trick you into thinking he was serious by "ring shopping", you are a lover of all things bright and beautiful so you shop for diamonds for yourself, or you enjoy window shopping with ya girls to educate yourselves on the wonderful possibilities/options in the form of diamonds. One thing that you've probably learned, and I believe we all can agree on, is that a single or solitaire diamond with a heavier carat weight is much more valuable than multiple tiny chips that are clustered together to simulate the look of an extraordinary 1, 2, or 3 carat stand-alone. You might be familiar with the 4 c's of the diamond:

Color, cut, clarity, and carat weight. So let me introduce you to the 4 C's of YOU, a highly valued single. First, your CUT. Despite what derogatory songs may say about your replicability or "on to next one themed songs". YOU ARE UNIQUE! Did you know that no one in the entire world has the same fingerprint as you? Not even you have a duplicate fingerprint from the left hand to the right hand...That was on purpose and by GOD's design. You are cut from a different cloth, EXCLUSIVE! I realize, and I hope you do as well, that not everyone will be in a romantic relationship or get married, but some have that desire and ultimately will. So is your worth based solely on you, or only when you're coupled? You ARE worthy whether you are in a relationship or not, whether you are married or single. God designed you to be born for a purpose, and that purpose is to be fulfilled while you are single and even more so when and if you do become married. Your value is NOT based on a relationship; it is based on your God-given purpose to be fulfilled while you are alive. As a matter of fact, the only relationship that determines a higher value is the one you begin or already have with GOD as his child.

"For you created my inmost being; you knit me together in my mother's womb. I praise you because I am fearfully and wonderfully made; your works are wonderful, I know that full well. My frame was not hidden from you when I was made in the secret place, when I was woven together in the depths of the earth. Your eyes saw my unformed body; all the days ordained for me were written in your book before one of them came to be." Psalm 139:13-16 (NIV)

"But you are a chosen people, a royal priesthood, a holy nation, God's special possession, that you may declare the praises of him who called you out of darkness into his wonderful light." 1 Peter 2:9 (NIV)

This relationship helps you determine the reason you were put here. The creator knows why He created you. It's your job to seek Him --- to find out what that is and get busy doing that. Some people begin to use drugs and or alcohol to cover the pain of not having a reason to live, for a higher purpose than themselves, or have become so burdened with the constant stresses of life, it not being what they expected. This can send some into a perpetual downward spiral, and they battle bouts of depression. According to the World Health Organization, Depression is the leading cause of disability worldwide and is a major contributor to the overall global burden of disease. Globally, more than 300 million people of all ages suffer from depression.

Know that whatever life brings, happiness, struggles, hardships, joy, feelings of unworthiness, know that you ARE valuable—you are to die for, and Christ did just that for YOU because he loves you like no other.

Begin by finding out your spiritual gifts, your purpose and how God can use them in you for his glory. This is not an exhaustive list, but something for you to think about:

1. Giving	7. Mercy
2. Healing	8. Prophecy
3. Helps	9. Serving
4. Hospitality	10. Discernment
5. Knowledge	11. Teaching (aka shepherding)
6. Leadership	12. Wisdom

Chapter 10
Let The Healing Begin

What is Healing? It is defined as the process of becoming sound or healthy again, or of becoming free from injury or disease. How many times have you been hurt by a relationship that was no good for you, toxic, or maybe you deliberately ran into a relationship to cover the hurt from the previous relationship, and never took the time to heal? The fact of the matter is that we could have had a relationship that perhaps would have just stayed in the friendship zone, or not even happened at all, if you had taken the time to become a whole person who let the work of healing begin in your physical, emotional, and spiritual selves. We all, as children, can remember scraping our knees, playing with friends, and getting an injury or a "boo-boo". We saw the blood from the cut eventually form over the once-opened wound and form a hard scab. Our parents typically warned us not to pick at it and to let it heal. But, as immature children, we didn't quite understand what that meant, so we let our curiosity get the best of us and played investigator. The scab may have healed around the edges, so we lifted it up to see what was underneath. Our tiny eyes saw that the skin that was once torn had mended, and the color slowly returned to normal, exactly where the scar could be lifted. Annoyance set in, when we saw that the edges beneath the scab were intact, but the center could not be lifted. Meaning that the center was not yet ready for the scab to let go, because healing was still taking place. Though our minds couldn't quite comprehend what was taking place as kids, we thought we'd speed that stage along. We picked, picked, picked, and picked until we eventually re-injured the wound, causing it to bleed and prolonging the healing process. We became somewhat angry that removing the scab before it was time DID NOT reveal pristine healed skin restored to its previous condition.

Here we are now, more mature, having gained experience that shows letting our center heal is the best way to achieve the best results. What is your center in this chapter of life? Your center is your heart, soul, mind, body, spirit, and emotions. How have you healed from the last relationship? Girl stop, and don't do the same thing expecting different results. Contrary to popular actions of the masses, there is no way to drown out not being a healed person with over-working, illicit sex, overeating, or a breakneck speed party lifestyle. It's the quiet moments when you write things down—attitudes, thought patterns, and actions you see that you don't like about yourself or the decisions you have made. Learning to pray, read the word of God, and connect with mature, positive people who will not take advantage of your vulnerability. Seeking out mentors and having tough conversations, or just listening to wise counsel. These are some healthy ways to heal while taking time alone, outside of any new relationships. Have you sought counseling? You need to learn from your past and burn the road that leads to backward thinking; be delivered from your old mindset that says you are ok WITHOUT doing the work it takes to heal your center and live in denial.

Let's not be fooled: you have to refuse to be set up by your enemy, the devil, to attack your center. If you have ever visited a gun range, seen a professional gun-man, military, special police, or tactical specialist shooting at a man-like figure on a paper target. "Shooting center mass offers a big target. The upper torso contains the lungs, heart, spine—things that if mutilated, severed, or destroyed would help stop someone intent on killing you."[1] Your center is of utmost importance to protect, because your vital organs are irreplaceable, and even if you could replace them, you might have to wait months or even years on a list to receive them. That's why it's so crucial that we protect the things that keep our center healthy, because if the heart is sick, the whole body is affected. Don't worry, however, no matter what stage you are in, Psalms reminds us that God:

"He heals the brokenhearted and binds up their wounds" Psalm 147:3 (NIV)

All we must do is keep seeking healing through credible, trustworthy sources and commit to doing the self-work. No one can change you or force you to admit that there are things that need changing within.

You are so valuable; you must list all the things about you that are unique. You have good character, love, self-love, kindness, value, morals, wisdom, and discipline. You don't have to discount any of those qualities to receive external

---

1. https://www.guns.com/news/2011/07/14/why-shoot-ce
   nter-mass

love from anyone. Cheapening yourself undermines the values that God has ascribed to us. He created you!! No one has the authority to edit your value. No matter how, you have to remind yourself to renew your mind, to rehearse what God has already said, and to avoid external forces, men looking to take advantage, negative self-talk, worry, or sorrow that could possibly penetrate the seal that God has placed over you. You are loved by the ultimate lover (Jesus Christ), and you are his prized possession.

Chapter 11

The Lust Trap: Intimacy Before Marriage

Sometimes I wish I could press the redo or restart button as it pertains to intimacy before marriage. All the times we thought we were so deeply in love, only to realize that we were blinded, ignoring all the tell-tale signs in great big neon letters with sirens saying **DANGER - DO NOT CROSS**. We naively crossed anyway, thinking that because we are special, different from any other woman (in which we are), that this would somehow prevent him from being attracted to having his cake and eating it too. And -- not giving you the emotional availability, time, or ambition you so desired to see in his "potential". We all have been duped in one way or another and realized that all the time, attention, caring, emotional struggle, and learning about the other person was a one-sided attempt at a relationship, if it was a real relationship at all. The totality of our disgust, hurt, mistrust, regret, at times bitterness/outrage that may turn to apathy all stem from one thing…being intimate with a person who did not share a covenant or make a vow to be there for us when the dust settled.

After the newness of the relationship wears off, you both face the fact that a relationship shows each person a mirror of who they really are. Intimacy before marriage, fools us into thinking the connection was stronger than it was because of two souls being joined together prematurely. And yet again we see that no amount of sex can change a person to be more faithful, to have more ambition, to love GOD, to deal with the emotional demons from their childhood, to set a plan for the future life they want to live, or be a father if he does not want children. *Sex* is often used as a cheap way to quicken a relationship into a pseudo-marriage. We sometimes aren't even sure if we desire to enter because we DON'T really KNOW the person we are with. We kick ourselves for being poor students of the sensible advice we give others about relationships. In essence, we have fallen into the LUST trap. We felt pressured by societal norms, loneliness, the mate we were in a relationship with, or the competition of the "Other thirsty women" supposedly lined up to give a man all the things he wants from a woman with no pressure to commit. We are in a major rush to get into the gate of the relationship, but once in, we see the stay is painfully long -- with no hope of change, so we keep plugging along, with the rationale that *all* the time we invest in doing the work of the relationship will be wasted. Not understanding that, staying longer while *he* enjoys the creature comforts, has only secured his win of your mind and body commitment without him doing any further self-improvement to win the prize, YOU—for him, the hunt is over, he is perhaps bored and not sure how to end it, because marriage was never the plan to begin with. Or for him not to end the relationship at all, but to continue receiving all the benefits you offer while doing whatever or whomever he wants, while you remain performative for the final level of commitment: marriage. Even if this is not your bag/experience, pick a variation of a disappointment level. The relationship plateaued at the expense of your body, soul, and spirit, contributing to the hurt you must overcome in the interim before you fully heal and meet the partner you will ultimately marry. Digging out from the physical, emotional, and spiritual rubble strewn across your psyche will be the hard work you must do, only with the help of God. Was it worth it? What you thought was love might have been, but was it reciprocated? The love you gave. Was it received as the lust...an offering to satisfy a yearning that couldn't wait until it was in its proper confines?

> Let marriage be held in honor among all, and let the marriage bed be undefiled, for God will judge the sexually immoral and adulterous. Hebrews 13:4 (ESV)

Going forward, we all tend to see our mistakes clearly. Accept it, do not overconsume yourself on past mistakes. God's grace covers you; there is forgiveness, healing, and hope for your future. Let's not continue to scold ourselves, but relish in God's liberating grace. Learn that the only thing that we must run from is the lust trap. Just as Joseph ran from Potiphar's wife, who chased him and wanted to sleep with him because he was handsome. He ran because the strength lust has is strong; we don't want to fool ourselves and play with fire. Those who know that they are healing or perhaps already transitioned into the state of *being* a healed, whole person, know that they deserve someone who does not rush intimacy. I have a journal, and in it I jotted the things I learned from my past relationships regarding intimacy and my future mate:

> -My values and morals are not for compromise (I am intended for my husband)

- If a man pushes me to compromise my morals and values (It's satanic)
- A true mate will protect my virtue
- My partner absolutely must be an equally yoked Christian
- Stop making my partner more important than my relationship with Christ
- I will no longer live with a man until I am officially married
- I must be a happy, whole person and meet other happy, whole people
- I don't need to tell a person I am dating that I am waiting for marriage; just do it.

Don't forecast a vow that is between you and God.

I also made notes of the differences between LOVE and LUST. So I could always flip back and remind myself what I learned:

LOVE	**LUST**
Is of God	Is of the world = popular opinion
Can wait = patient	Must have it now = impatient
Selfless	Selfish
Giving	Takes constantly or wants to know what's in for me (Transactional)
Willing to sacrifice, costly Jesus sacrificed his life	Doesn't want to sacrifice Free love mindset
Encourages purity	Encourages sin, compromises morals and values
Develops	Destroys (I want it now, I don't care who it hurts)
Peaceful	Anxiety inducing
Meets biblical standards	Directly contradicts scriptures

Showing your cards too early or mentioning what you have in your hand in a spades game will have your team fast on their way to "being set." For those who don't play spades, this is when you're well on your way to losing the game. We women sometimes have a bit of an ego too, and to avoid being preyed on by a lustful man, we announce every chance we get to any potential suitor that will listen, "That we are waiting until marriage to be intimate". That, in fact, can turn a man away, a man who initially had lust as the primary attraction, but with time would have fallen in love with you as a person. I feel that we women who are indeed trying to wait, sometimes use this phrase as a weapon to scare off men we believe would not be suitable for us. Perhaps we don't realize that we are just to live out our lives and not be so preachy with our words. To understand fully that men respond to our actions of denying lustful sexual advances more than lip service about what we would do if the opportunity presented itself. Let's remember the New Year, when we perhaps set goals to reduce or eliminate certain foods. Then, as the year progressed and social gatherings commenced, the aroma of the very food item we had been steadfastly avoiding wafted. Mind you, no one from our previous interaction when we first made the public or private declaration is around at the moment. Then we cleverly commence to making our plate, only to include what we clearly said we would avoid.

Lesson:

Lust is very subtle, and our pride can have us women thinking that if we make a declaration to someone of what we will not do before marriage, that this makes us "bulletproof", if you will, to the powerful vortex of lust. We must learn to keep our vow to God and ourselves without pronouncing to the world, because when we believe we can do things in our own strength and self-righteousness, which is exactly when we stumble. Proverbs 16:18 says, "Pride goes before destruction, a haughty spirit before a fall."

I find that journaling is important to me at times, because my future stepchild, Godchild, or mentee can go back and read the thought processes I had throughout my life. Also, if and when you decide that the time is right to begin dating again, you can take your time and observe the person who has expressed an interest in you carefully. Take notes, and ask yourself and him questions. Try not to let emotions make decisions for you. Is this person genuine, or are they saying the things you want to hear to reach a short-term goal of sleeping with you? Don't inform him of what you want; it's easy for him to repeat back that same script you've given him. Ask him what he wants. What are *his* life goals and vision? Ask the hard questions! Avoid getting caught up in the physical, overly flirtatious stuff that leads nowhere fast. Search his mind, because if nothing is there now, there will most likely be nothing there later. It's *not* your job to make him ready for something outside of a physical relationship; it *is* your job not to be so hungry that you accept or eat lies to fulfill your need for companionship. You are a whole person, you don't have to rush! You are intelligent enough to make calculated decisions by evaluating character, asking probing questions, and verifying who this person really is through *true*, trustworthy friends.

Chapter 12
Stop Being So Available

The definition of easy according to Webster's dictionary is, "A: causing or involving little difficulty or discomfort, within easy reach. B: requiring or indicating little effort, thought, or reflection; easy clichés."[1] Looking back on my own experiences and reintroducing myself to the thoughts of my father, who was married to my mother for 52 years before my mom passed in February of 2025: Men (in the western culture) almost never commit to easy choices. That easy choice is being a woman who presents little or no difficulty to a man who strategically gathers information about what that woman desires (mostly through

---

1. Easy Definition of Easy by Merriam-Webster https:// www.merriam-webster.com/dictionary/eas

her telling him). HE pretends he desires the same thing, conquers, and leaves. It's simple to fall victim to going with the flow or doing what every other woman is doing and think that, in some sort of crazy definition of insanity, that doing the same thing with men, will somehow get you different results. No matter how hard the stings of loneliness hit, that sting is most preferable rather than the destruction of your mind, body, and soul because you gave in too soon. Your dignity is always worth more than keeping a companion and compromising your values. We women, don't want to believe it, but men don't want to commit because they DON'T have to. Collectively, women in previous years only gave up marriage privileges (sex, cooking, cleaning, overnight companionship, and financial help) to people with whom they entered into a marriage relationship. Men collectively could not, on a widespread basis, have sex with several random women, without most of the time being in a covenant marriage relationship. This is by no means a hard-and-fast rule. Plenty of people were in marriage relationships and stepped out on their mates, but statistics show that people married younger and actually valued marriage, rather than shacking up or living in with their mate. These days, men laugh while reaping all the benefits of marriage without fear of any of the financial repercussions of a breakup. They can walk away 'Scott free' without owing their mate anything, financially, emotionally, spiritually, or otherwise. It was a mere hook-up, boyfriend/girlfriend transaction.

No matter what mistakes you have made in the past, make a vow to yourself that you won't be easy. You are too valuable to always be readily available to people who don't want to make the sacrifice to get to know the *real* you. You manifest greatness, so if you keep attracting people who want you to discount yourself to be with them, *RUN*. Don't be so convenient, don't fit in, stand out. You are not common, something that anybody can have and handle in any way *they* deem suitable to *them* in a relationship, friendship, or otherwise. It's tempting to think that settling for less will give you a win. Retrain your thinking. Meeting someone and putting your all into being a good friend while they barely respond is not a good investment, because you need someone who is willing to put the same amount of energy into you that you will put into them. Your morals, values, respect, and your personhood mustn't be discounted. As a woman who is 100% guilty of this in the past, it's time we all collectively put our foot down and say no more.

Let me tell you a story about a woman in a pseudo-relationship with an older man. She was in her early 30s, and he was in his early 50s. Upon meeting him in a seminary class where she was learning the history of international missionary work, as well as strategies on effective missionary relations between the local church and the countries in which they serve. She had an instant attraction to this man's spirit when he entered the room, even before she saw him. Later, as he sat on the edge of the room, she realized he was about to be introduced as the teacher/pastor for that week's lessons. As time progressed during the various weeks of the teaching designated to one instructor, the class had several tasks. During group assignments where the class had to do specific group discussions with as many as 8 or more persons at an assigned table, he would approach and call her by name, which was impressive to her because, having at least 40 or more persons in the room, to her meant that there was effort applied to remember her name specifically. As he taught the class and interacted with her, she felt such a strong connection with him that she took the liberty to reach out to him via email.

This was the start of the secret relationship, where all her friends and family knew she was seeing only him, but the reverse was not true for him. She found herself driving long hours to another state to see him frequently and come to parties where she was never introduced as anything other than her first name (not girlfriend or Lady Friend), even among his family members. Now, this went on for quite some time, with her traveling out of her state to him and him traveling out of his state to her, which may have taken up to an hour or 2. Only to be treated like she didn't exist until after all his house guests were gone or the event ended, then and only then, they were actually together. Despite his behavior, she remained readily available to someone who knew her eagerness and strong desire to be with him, which allowed him to keep their dealings secret. He could do the exact same thing with someone else, or be a different person around one set of people and be a whole different person while they were together. She was too available to someone who *was* unwilling to publicly commit to a relationship. She drove for long hours and supported him in public settings, where she was reluctantly acknowledged, if at all.

After several months of this pattern, she woke up and realized that this man's public persona and private persona (character) were not the same, therefore unworthy of giving any more time and attention. She realized she was worth more and did not have to be so available to a person who was not willing to fully commit to a public relationship. Her over availability cost her emotionally, spiritually, and financially. Let's learn the lesson: not to give our all and receive scraps from others; you are worth the sacrifice.

Chapter 13
The Safety of Wise Counselors

Where *there is* no counsel, the people fall; but in the multitude of counselors *there is* safety.
Proverbs 11:14 (KJV)

It's hard nowadays to meet someone we are attracted to, actually like their personality, have things in common, and are mutually complementary (opposite strengths). We, who are trying our best to keep our private life private in the age of social media, and to have some semblance of control over what the world can influence in our day-to-day lives, at times find it complex. It is easy to turn inwards in a cancel culture that promotes cutting people off at the least and sometimes the most petty disagreement or varying viewpoint. We may find ourselves now, whisked away into a very fast-moving fairytale relationship. Wherein the guy is so charming, says all the right things, and treats us so well. This causes us to dive into the relationship at breakneck speed, not at all showing this person to our friends or loved ones so they can get a closer look and offer some words of wisdom. We now find ourselves on an island, all alone with our new love interest in a pseudo marriage. Blocking out the world, ignoring all the red flags or warnings that this can't last. Nevertheless, it's just you and bae. This is a dangerous equation: if you don't learn your partner thoroughly, and he knows you are willing to abandon all your other relationships with family and friends just to be with him. He knows now he's got you right where he wants you...all alone. In the scenario, you feel comfortable, not knowing the emotional pain you will go through, this is all a part of a simple strategy to isolate you and have you second-guessing your decisions because you have no one to consult with. There is a sense of shame in venturing out to ask whether you are doing the right things in certain matters after you willingly made trite decisions on your own. You feel trapped. Living with someone is a huge step, and now, in hindsight, you realize the decision to do so has left you feeling more alone *in* a relationship than you would be without. The person that you are with seems to purposely social distance themselves from their family and friends. No one is invited to their home. You are now in a social vacuum. Your only interaction is limited to your partner and a few of your friends you see on the outside. This island has become a place you need to break free from to get counsel, to vent to others about your experience, and to plan a way of escape. Desperation, and over-eagerness to be in a relationship, that you had no idea that you were exhibiting traits of, has landed you smack dab in the middle of a rash decision.

Before this incident, you were in the safety of singles groups, Christian dating classes, or among other singles who were carefully navigating a Godly life. Now you begin to pray and seek friends who can advise you on how to make it work or to get out. Seeking help to right the wrongs by going to pre-marital counseling, pushing the bad decision even further into the abyss of fitting a square peg into a round hole.

After reading the Bible, getting grounded in the word, watching Christian YouTube videos, and seeking counsel from wise male and female friends who have successfully navigated the waters of single life and who are now happily married or happily single, you finally regain your focus. You come to a profound realization that before this event, you managed to stay on track, not because you were so perfect, but because the entire time of your singleness, you were under strong biblical teaching; you were connected to others in your age group who were going through similar circumstances, and the conversations strengthened you to not give up. Once those safety measures disappeared, there was a sense of isolation that can put an invisible target on your back to those looking to destroy people whose wills are becoming weak from the long wait. Just like any herd of animals, maybe wildebeest, the pack is much more threatening than a single animal that wanders out alone, dazed and confused. The key is not to find just any group but a godly group, because an ungodly group can motivate you in negative ways that can also prove to be destructive. But, to find a group that is willing to uphold the standard of God, no matter how off-trend or corny the mainstream deems it. They, and you alike, will not be easily manipulated into a follower mentality; To the contrary, they will hold themselves in high regard by following as best they can God's handbook on dealing with the temptations and misgivings of the single life. As iron sharpens iron, so one man or woman, for that matter, sharpens another according to the scripture passage found in Proverbs 27:17. The takeaway is not everybody is considered iron, so you must choose your counselors wisely. Safely landing yourself in a support system, whether that be a church family, close godly friends, or even married couples who have taken up the spiritual mantle to help singles with godly guidance. Beware of going against your better judgment, spiritual discernment, and biblical counsel.

It never fails that after a toxic relationship, we blind ourselves from seeing all the negative aspects and hone in on good times only, even if those so-called "nice times" were not even real. Sometimes we can be naïve to the point where the man can use his representative to get on our good side in the preliminary. Showing us all the things we want in a man, then those actions evaporate into a mist of verbal degradation. We leave the relationship and may step back from dating for a while to heal, grow wiser and stronger, and work on our character. Only to fall victim to loneliness, regressing and falling backwards, reaching out to the Ex, who was an ex for a reason. You may perhaps reach out to someone who is married, or in the health field for advice, in a scramble for someone to tell you to come to your senses and move forward in victory to wait on the one whom God has designed for you. In this instance, you are instructed against your better judgment (from bad counsel) to reach out and open a chapter that has been long closed for some time. You take the advice because there is a curious part of you that wants to know if he has changed and is willing to give it another go. Once you speak to him, you realize that the verbal digs and blame game haven't changed much at all; older doesn't always mean wiser or more mature. You see the same games played now; it only takes a couple of weeks to see the interest is not there, but the counsel was not wise and has put you smack dab in the middle of the cycle you got out of the first place. We are much too old at this point in our lives to beg or wait for someone to come around and love and care for us. We are much too precious, worth more than rubies; our self-respect must be high enough to bear some of the stings of being single, while we enjoy the peace it provides. Our relationship must be so close with God that we can hear him, over the noise of those who have not been delivered by God of behaviors so toxic, that it had to be something from Satan himself.

Chapter 14

I'm Tired of Waiting: The Patience Game

Sharing my own experiences with being single for the better part of my life, currently 45 years to be exact, save for a few fly-by-night 6 months or less relationships or a bit more. I have found that patience is one of THE hardest virtues while waiting. As an African-American woman who considers herself well-traveled, cultured, open-minded to a large degree, and adventurous, there are unique circumstances that seem to surround our community that still exist in others, but to a much lesser degree. We in the African American culture experience extremely high rates of singleness and among the highest rates of unwed mothers in America, tipping the scales at almost a whopping 80% of unmarried black mothers are with children.

It has become all too familiar to be a relatively successful woman on paper, and lack the desired prospect of a committed relationship that ends in marriage. Some women have chosen to focus their minds on other things, like their career goals, traveling the world, going back to school for advanced degrees, teaching English in a foreign country, starting their own business, or purposefully planning to adopt kids and become a single parent as their childbearing years wane. The stagnation of successful relationships that lead toward marriage has most women left wanting, myself included.

For those who do have the patience to wait and not become a part of the "statistics," we are all too often bemoaned to hear the clichés from friends and relatives. "When you're not looking for someone, that's when it will happen for you", "Maybe you're just too picky", "Maybe your standards are too high", "Oh, you don't have a boyfriend or husband?!... What's wrong with you? "Are you gay?" "You still haven't found someone you like?" "You should be more social." "Have you traveled?" "Have you tried meeting someone at church?" "Have you tried approaching a man?" Have you tried online dating apps? I heard of a few people who've found their spouse on them." You should come to this event or that event...blah, blah, blah. This enters one ear and goes right out the other.

Why? Because most women who have had the luxury of being single or single without children have traveled to several countries and umpteen states. Went to hundreds of gatherings, used multiple dating apps. They were introduced to someone by a friend or were promised to someone, but it never materialized. They've been speed dating, no dating, slow dating, and cold dating. They've dated in a tree, they've dated in a car, they've dated near, and they've dated far. They dated when it's cold, they've dated when it's hot; at this point, it really doesn't matter who they've dated or not... none of them worked!!

It's bothersome because most people who are comfortably in a relationship, and those in marriages, soon forget the experience of being single, or even being happily single and still wanting a mate. It gets a bit draining to keep putting yourself out there to people who say they are going to call or make promises to connect. You fall into the text vortex of the dreaded copy and paste "Good morning, beautiful", "WYD" (what you doing?), or the ever-so-intellectual "Hi" 10 times in a row with no response from you. You're lulled into being somewhat content and free from the emptiness of hollow dating without a purpose or intention. Trying to gauge your expectations while still keeping your character, morals, and values intact. You tire from it all, bobbing and weaving through half-hearted attempts to capture your emotions, to barely any hearted. You know the, "Throw the net into water guys" who put out the least possible amount of effort with multiple women, to see if they take the cheap pieces of chum inside the net and be taken in as their catch.

Some have prayed for years or decades to meet a godly man who was attractive and willing to court them. At times, I must admit it seems like a curse on the African American community or some sort of willful design that the family is perpetually destroyed. Fathers have no interest in marrying or sticking around to raise kids, but are pushed to fill some quota of impregnating multiple women, and complain about a system that was never designed to have peaceful resolutions. Discipline is often thrown out the window as it relates to love and loyalty to one mate for a lifetime. Women who attempt to make themselves better via therapy to heal wounds from the past, be it from family or failed relationships, have the hard work of choosing from those who think their wounds are not deep enough for therapy. Or that the constant, everlasting hustle for money and notoriety will somehow dissipate years of childhood trauma from cycles of fatherless homes with single mothers struggling to provide, teach, and discipline kids. Women often pay attention to the details painted into patterns of how the generational cycles keep revolving and strain with all their might to put an end to them. But how can she do it alone? It's a very heavy burden to carry. Heck, even Jesus left the earth after 33 years of being a single man, going about his father's business. So, for those longing to return to a time when marriage created generational wealth through education and when two parents nurtured children by being walking, talking, breathing examples. Most women are left unfulfilled. They've done everything society and the church have, heck, even the bible says to do, but don't see a road to a loving relationship after they've done the work. Some women have reached the pinnacle of their careers and opted to forge ahead as single mothers, hoping that this relationship would fulfill their need to give love.

"A hope deferred makes the heart grow sick, but a longing fulfilled is the tree of life" (Proverbs 13:12). If you are at the point where you feel things may never happen for you, and your patience has almost evaporated. Please don't feel like you're alone. It would be foolish to say that everyone is perfect and never experiences frustration. If you have not been called by God to live a permanent life of singlehood, it is ok to want a mate. You shouldn't be made to feel guilty about it because it's a natural desire placed inside of you by God himself. If you have filled your heart with Christ Jesus and have a personal relationship with him, then there is a longing that God has allotted to only be filled by him, AND a space that only a mate can fulfill. That is what God set as an example in Genesis.

As the world had transformed into a global quarantine, it gave us much time to think and notice we are not designed to be isolated our entire lives. As a single, I still long for the intimacy of someone to hold me, hug me, grab my hand, and talk to me closely in my ear. I desire the touch of a special man, not just any man, but the one who will dedicate himself to me and me only. A man who is not blind to the fact that other beautiful women exist, but is so loyal that he chooses to still be with me, to enjoy the ups and downs of life. I'd be lying if I said I don't long for a fulfilling relationship that leads to marriage, with a man that I am totally attracted to, all while still enjoying a completely fulfilling single life. I think its okay to say that we are enjoying our lives as singles and still have a desire for a mate. The peril is rushing into something just to satisfy a desire; you'll end up back in the repair shop of therapy and self-reflection so fast that you will regret being hasty and impatient.

Chapter 15
Avoiding The Popularity Contest

High school is probably the best example of when you, as a teenager, wanted to fit in and be accepted by your peers so badly, to feel a sense of belonging. If you stroll down memory lane, you'll remember the popular girls seemed to wear all the latest fashions and hairstyles, while having all the guys who were considered handsome or "pretty boys" in their friend circle. To you, they all seemed to say the right things, and maybe you were part of that group, but if you were not, you may have strived to find ways to be accepted to no avail. So after all the failed attempts to be more like someone else, you, by default, started being yourself. For me, that was being the girl who loved to be athletic and play sports, as I often did growing up as a tomboy, hanging out with my brother. So, in high school, whether that was playing basketball, wrestling, and track, or, to throw in the assortment of my love for music/arts, being a member of the choir, I was seen as weird. I didn't find much in common with the average girl. So I was a natural loner. As time went on, I didn't really listen to what most of my friends, who were mostly outside of school, said about being popular and fitting in. Sleeping with guys seemed to be their prescribed way to be accepted. After a few failed, empty, and hollow experiences, I determined that this was fruitless.

Fast forwarding to adulthood, most people's perspectives haven't changed all that much but has been almost reinforced that to be happy so to speak, you must go along with the crowds of people settling for cohabitation, children out-of-wedlock, casual sex, open relationships and entanglements of the like, along with all the diseases, broken family structures and mental health havoc that comes along with them. You're considered old-fashioned, crazy, stubborn, and an oddball if you believe a relationship is defined as two people committed to each other and each other alone who both value marriage, walking toward it in a reasonable time frame, sans dating into perpetuity, and will commit to be one hundred percent faithful to one another. Otherwise, what's the point of being in a relationship if there is no commitment? You both can live as two single, *separate* people, doing whatever each pleases, with no one to answer to but God, and the kids who are a product of these relationships will see the living example of what *you* think is a model relationship.

This time around, as an adult, the stakes have risen higher in the superficial aspect. We are now in the age of the Instagram model who flaunts lips, butts, and boobs to thirsty followers. The goal of relationships is confusing to most. Woman have changed their whole look and persona to please men's pornographic fantasy, but the state of friendships or relationships hasn't improved; it's actually gotten a lot worse. There is still hope! The goal is to avoid the pitfalls of the popular social constructs. Placing all of your personal business on social media, overindulging in parading a newly found mate on the internet for social approval. Or turning into a thirst trap because you see that there are 'slim pickens', so you become influenced by the crowd that shows all the men, you have the goods. It's so hard to just exist and be happy without feeling you need to do what everyone else is doing to win. Most people are afraid to be different and are judged by the very same people who say that others are judging them. You are called politically correct because you choose to be different. Value, honesty, and integrity have never been accepted in a world filled with a dog-eat-dog, get-them-before-they-get-you mentality. How can you avoid the incessant need to join the popularity contest? Seek the truth and virtue within you, seek the Holy Spirit to comfort you when the conviction to do the right has you feeling that you're missing out on something. Seeking the comfort of God when doing the right thing will have you walking alone. Also, be grateful to God that your path of reward will be different from the same people who you felt were succeeding by doing the wrong things.

> "Be still before the LORD and wait patiently for Him; fret not when men prosper in their ways, when they carry out wicked schemes". Psalm 37:7 (ESV)

Your blessings will be greater in this life and the next. Your blessings will have longevity, not that of short-lived passions and pleasures that those who choose to do evil willfully have only for a short time.

> The blessing of the LORD, it maketh rich, and he addeth no sorrow with it. Proverbs 10:22 (KJV)

No matter the blessing you receive in life, whether that is a mate in marriage, spiritual peace, mental restoration, or financial blessings, you won't have to look over your back in paranoia with your blessings, or it won't be someone else's husband. You will enjoy the blessing in peace, knowing that God has, through his perfect provision, graced you with a sorrow-free blessing.

Stay the course of the narrow road; it's worth the wait.

Chapter 16

No Romance Without Finance

"Ain't Nothin' Goin' on But The Rent" is a controversial hit song recorded by late R&B recording artist Gwen Guthrie, released as a single in 1986. Where in her lyrics she mentions a man must have a J-O-B to be with her, not be unemployed because there is no romance without finance.

As we women reach a certain stage of our lives where we have studied and graduated with school loans to boot, or maybe we went straight into entrepreneurship, with hard work plus dedication, we have scaled or are scaling a successful business. Perhaps you worked a 9 to 5 or as an independent contractor who stayed diligent with a side hustle after work hours, to now find yourself in a place in life where you are somewhat comfortable, maybe not rich or wealthy by any stretch of the imagination or maybe so (congrats) but at a place where you can't afford to have someone else pull you down to lift them up. Relishing yourself as the sacrificial lamb to "help a brother out" (*Especially* one that's not your husband) is **not** an option with your level of self-love and self-respect. Yes, this is something our parents did before they were married, back in the day, about 40 years ago. Two (young) people with nothing starting out worked their way up together; yes, which was a great recipe. Notice I said two people, not one with absolutely nothing to contribute. Let's examine how cake recipes have changed over the last four decades, with different ingredients, a more scrumptious taste, easier preparation, and greater affordability. Are relationships as simple as cake batter? By no means, but there are better ways of doing things as time progresses. We have transitioned out of a society where the vast majority of women stayed home without "working" and took the ever so difficult task of working the *same* jobs, raising kids, cooking, cleaning, keeping up with the education of the children, all while being the positive encouragement to her husband and his refuge from the cruel world, still "Work". Of which, if we had a line item total in today's currency, it would be an almost 6-figure salary to hire someone else to complete these tasks (*and* the part you can't quantify is **the love** and **patience** that goes a long way in the process). Many people can attest to paying babysitters or daycare workers for the maltreatment of their children while they were forced to work to make a living. Women are now free to choose a life that includes careers, and some have had to forge ahead, raising kids as single moms while working, which often complicates the dynamics of their relationships.

Where does this leave the woman? She is often burdened with various responsibilities that entail a financial obligation. When I was a young woman, at the ripe age of 22, I remember how hard and smart I had to work to purchase my first home. I avoided clubbing, I never gambled nor had the desire, I wasn't a drinker, so I wasn't poppin' bottles on the weekend, I didn't have all the latest fashion trends and thrifted most times, and I barely even traveled. I sacrificed seeing all my clients leave on vacations to Essence music festivals, some said they were heading to this Caribbean island, and that. All while I worked to drum up clientele working as an independent contractor with two jobs, one as a personal trainer in Laurel, Maryland, and the other as a nutritionist at a local children's hospital in Washington, D.C., to make the desired money I needed to pay rent and save for a home. Why? Because I so desperately despised apartment living, with its jammed flats, intolerable noise levels, and random people who smoked above or below that would billow into the vents, up on the patio, when my windows weren't even open. I wanted my own detached home, and God blessed me with that dream at 22.

Women are now career-driven *and* homemakers. We must not let a man or the desperation of wanting to be with one derail us from being fiscally responsible. A man who is referred to in the biblical sense, when he is ready to be with a woman in a serious manner, is commanded to work. This song above is not about gold-digging, it's about goal-digging! In the African American community, we have dropped the ball for several generations to create wealth to be handed down to our children's children according to the scripture in Proverbs 13:22. Some of which is not entirely our fault due to our forefathers constantly under attack when they did, their entire wealthy communities were burned down to the ground. But now we must take responsibility and act with wisdom to play catch-up, purposing that we will not leave this earth until we have something to hand down to our children besides debt.

A woman carries a lot of burdens on her shoulders, and she doesn't need another from a grown man who won't contribute. Let me be absolutely clear. A man is not required to pay your bills when you are dating. However, if the man doesn't even have money to pay his portion of a Dutch date, why would you consider him for a relationship or marriage? As a woman, you have to have the same qualities that you desire in your mate. If you are financially stable, it's not highway robbery to want a gentleman who makes that his priority as well, has taken the necessary steps to get there, and has *something* to contribute. Just as the song says, "nothing from nothing leaves nothing". Some of us women, not all, truly, lower our standards and become quite desperate for a warm body; some will accept any stray bird, who will willingly lay up and receive all the benefits of being with you, with not an iota of responsibility. I experienced this when I became a landlord years ago of that same house I bought and later moved out to rent. I chose Section 8 housing for my home, to provide struggling mothers with a quality place to live while they are assisted by the state-run program. Mind you, I had the option of renting to doctors from Europe and other high-income earners, so this was a decision, not an obligation. When I came to collect the rent, she was late or unable to pay, all while mentioning her boyfriend was sleeping in the home that reeked of cigarettes and weed, which was not allowed (I was informed by the neighbors he was actually living there on and off). Now, ladies, how in the world can you let a man live in the house and can't help you pay $200 to cover the entire rent bill? That's right, the rent was exactly $200! So I'm guessing he wasn't paying for food either because she was on food stamps, which meant she had an additional dependent in the household outside of her 2 children she took care of, HIM!

There is a bible scripture that speaks of the men who do not want to work in these ways:

> But if anyone does not provide for his relatives, and especially for members of his household, he has denied the faith and is worse than an unbeliever. 1 Timothy 5:8 (ESV)

> For even when we were with you, we would give you this command: If anyone is not willing to work, let him not eat. 2 Thessalonians 3:10 (ESV)

> The Lord God took the man and put him in the Garden of Eden to work it and keep it. Genesis 2:15 (ESV)

We, as ladies, must be grounded in the principles of the word of God, knowing that God wants to give you the desires of your heart, but we can't settle for less because we get fatigued by the wait. We are dating to find out the pertinent information; don't get blinded by looks, glittering cars, or even flashy clothes. Yes, even this can be a trap. Take it from my experience: many years ago, I began dating a man who seemed to have it all together. Very nice high-end luxury vehicle that costs the price of a house, a home that was way too big for a single person with no kids, no visiting family members, or friends, to a 5-bedroom house. Very little to no furniture in a house that had been occupied for well over 3 years. This, to me, was a red flag: a man who was a decade and change older than me, who golfed every chance he could, only had one bed in the entire house and a couple of couches. I thought, "Dude can't afford this", because if he could, there would be signs of him furnishing it for family and friends, but most importantly himself.

I began trying to furnish his place (an ill-advised decision when you're trying to fulfill a role you haven't been given... wife). I'm thinking that if you can afford a car that costs as much as a house but can't furnish your place in under 4 years, that's a problem. But I, trying to be a fixer, wanted to come in and wave a magic wand over a man that wouldn't even be mine in the long run. So, ladies, just because he has a good job, a nice vehicle, and a home doesn't mean that man is financially compatible with you. If you were to get into a serious relationship with someone who couldn't travel, he has zero savings for his retirement at 50 plus, says he can't afford to have kids, but that is a desire of yours, can barely take you on dates (outside of the house), seems hamstrung to everything that pertains to treating you like the Queen you are, because they are over burdened with all the debts of trying to impress everyone in society with how they appear, let this be a careful decision. Some people are looking for someone to come into their life to help them, and they will use you as a resource to get what they want and need. They will rinse and repeat shortly after with a new and unsuspecting supply. You must know your financial goals before you begin dating. Are you working to be debt-free? Then it's not wise to date someone who is burdened with debt, does not care where their money goes, and spends $5000 at a club on the weekend on drinks and food, which is their way of having a good time, but they complain about tight finances throughout the remainder of the week, this a direct sign that you two are incompatible. There is a happy medium: a man who keeps a budget. By that, I mean he knows where every dollar goes each month and has even budgeted for dates, his future by putting some away, and for emergencies.

Chapter 17

Don't Be A Side Chick

Side chick is an American slang term used to define a woman who assumes a mistress role, at times unknowingly, in full or partial knowledge of another woman who is considered the main chick. "The Side Chick" typically participates in extracurricular activities, friends with benefits (sex), and the like. There are men who know that they themselves are more desirable as a married man; there is a sense of security that some feel a man has when he has settled down and has a family, a wife, and is seen by society as established. The man finds it exciting because there is an element of craftiness or sneakiness paired with the chance that they might get caught, which heightens the adrenaline of this extramarital or extra-curricular relationship. The man is not necessarily hiding the fact that he is married with children, and he is the provider to support whatever his family needs. He may tout himself as the good guy that everyone depends on; extended family members reach out to him for advice or perhaps financial assistance. He might simply mention he has a small child with a woman, but won't come out and say he is living with her. We have to be smarter and simply ask yes-or-no questions. Are you married, yes or no? Instead, he plays the role of the dependable and trusty man who just wants to be your friend and give you advice from time to time. It seems innocent enough, right? You can casually meet for lunch to talk business or to meet some influential people who are used as strategic pawns to impress you even further and solidify a desire inside of you to be close to power, influence, and opportunities. All powered by your plutonic friend who has your best interest at heart, or so it seems. In our western society, it is more of a taboo for a married man to be creeping around with a new woman who has struck his interest; it might be someone at work whom he encounters on a regular basis, or someone who has struck his fancy while he was out at a lunch meeting, and their eyes met. Regardless of how the chance meeting happened, there is now an urge for that man to conquer, like a hunter, what he desires. Some women are of the mindset that anything goes, and once a man makes an advance on her, whether he is married or not, it's fair game. She sees how he is dressed and perhaps draws all the context clues that he is well off, which could be beneficial for her (especially in poorer countries where upwards of 85% live three or four times below the poverty line of most Americans). Some spot a man's vehicle and wait for him to come into a restaurant so they can coincidentally bump into him.

Most times, the woman would not even be interested in him if it were based on just physical attraction, but in this case, money helps. It's actually kind of sick to think that a woman who desires healthy relationships and marriage would infiltrate someone else's relationship, fully knowing that there is another woman. To have that little regard for yourself and others is the exact reason why the world has become so cold-hearted, cruel, and self-absorbed. We, as women, need to remember that as we progress through life, we will find ourselves in the same positions as the people we disregard if we are not careful. That which you sow, that you shall also reap. Yes, the *man* has chosen not to honor his vows; for you to willfully participate further destroys the family unit, and you have become an advocate for that destruction. The women who participate in these behaviors hold men to such a low standard. Essentially, giving him everything he wants with little to no effort. It also hurts the women who refuse to settle for scraps or the term called "bread crumbing," where the man gives the scantiest effort, seeing if he can win women over to give him all the things he pleases without much attachment.

Ladies, *is it that hard*? Don't get me wrong, no one is perfect, and sometimes we get frustrated in the waiting process for "the one". No matter what you feel like you deserve as a "good woman," you don't deserve someone else's husband. There are consequences to pay for that sin if you decide to go on with your plans.

Hebrews 13:4 (ESV) says, "Let marriage be held in honor among all, and let the marriage bed be undefiled, for God will judge the sexually immoral and adulterous."

This side chick situation is an entirely different beast in African countries. I got a chance to understand the intricacies of this cultural practice by living in very close proximity to those who practiced it, some with their wives' knowledge and others without, but the wife seemed to have a gut feeling that it was happening because it is a cultural norm. For close to a year, I lived in Nairobi, Kenya. As I networked and traveled the country with all types of men doing business side by side for months, I had very limited interaction with other women. "The predominant religion in Kenya is Christianity, which is adhered to by an estimated 85.52% of the total population. Islam is the second largest religion in Kenya, practiced by 10.91 percent of Kenyans."[1] Most of them believe in marriage, as it is a part of their tribal traditions to get married fairly young and have children. What is unspoken to most outsiders is that the deep tribalism here has a public, but very veiled, part of the wedding ceremony: the woman basically agrees to have woman friends join her in the marriage, and the man has options of other women in the marriage. This is public knowledge among people of the culture who have been to many traditional gatherings and have lived within cultures practiced for decades before the arrival of colonial powers. As the saying goes, old habits and traditions are hard to break. I found myself sticking out like a sore thumb as I tried to exit from these same notions that have seeped deeply into Western culture. Where the new trend is that man is the prize, not the other way around. Imagine if you were a part of a handful of people who believe only single people are available to other single non-married people, compared to millions of people who believe that all is fair game once you leave your partner's presence. It reminds me of the scripture Matthew 7:12-14:

---

1. https://en.wikipedia.org/wiki/Religion_in_Kenya

"12 in everything, then, do to others as you would have them do to you. For this is the essence of the Law and the Prophets. 13 Enter through the narrow gate. For wide is the gate and broad is the way that leads to destruction, and many enter through it. 14 But small is the gate and narrow the way that leads to life, and only a few find it." (NIV)

This thought was so ingrained in the minds of men in Kenya that my friend from the UK and I, from the USA, who endeavored to start her own event in Kenya for singles to meet and network, found this indeed an obstacle. As I assisted her with the marketing campaign for her first event, we traveled to nice restaurants to chat about the event during peak lunch and happy hour times, then to local bars that had recently opened, with a later curfew of 11 pm in Nairobi during the COVID-19 pandemic. Men outright told us that there is no such thing as a single man in Kenya. Most guys drank their beers and laughed hysterically like we were the butt of the joke. However humiliated they thought we would be by the masses disagreeing with us, we did not budge on what we believed and stood for. We were of the mindset that you, as a man, can believe what you want and subscribe to whatever makes you feel better about cheating on your significant other, that because your values are skewed, every single person in their country did not adhere to those same thought standards.

Later, I actually got into a very deep conversation with a tall, super slim, chocolate-skinned Kenyan guy named Derek. He briefly told me about his past relationship and that he is 100% faithful and hasn't been back in a committed relationship for quite a while. Derek was very much my junior by 10 years, and he let me in on the little secret of what all the men thought of me once we exited the car to approach the restaurant...the typical guy banter as guys sit and drink their beer. Which part of a woman's body do they like the most, blah, blah, blah. But past that part, he shared that he was trying to release himself from the bondage of sex before getting to know a woman. This was so refreshing because he was in direct, total opposition to the other boisterous guy, who seemed to be the pack leader, loud, funny, and commanding. A pilot, Mike was his name, the one who thought that the idea of a singles event in Nairobi was completely ridiculous. Here you have direct evidence from this real story of my travel, that if 80% of people believe you have to be a side chick, there is still 20% that don't and would be willing to truly date seriously for the purpose and consideration of a faithful marriage between two people, minus any side dishes, snacks, or side chicks.

Chapter 18

Business or Booty Call?

Some call Kenya the "Wild West" of East Africa. The explanation is that there are literally no rules in relationships, business, traffic, or anything else. There is no structured way to do a background check on a person or businesses, save for googling articles, checking their status with the chamber of commerce, asking around to see if anyone else has had any dealings with them or reaching out to colleagues for some insights they could share about the business they have done with a private or public company in the past. So, just like the Wild West movies, anything goes; it's not even unheard of for people to disappear, be killed, and kidnapped over bad business deals or at the thought that someone can make a quick dollar off an unsuspecting newly wealthy victim.

In the west, there were few women who played shoot 'em up bang, bang with the boys, so an attractive dame trying to do business in the male-dominated territory is seen as easy pickings to some; they plan to use her in business and perhaps fulfill their sexual fantasy simultaneously. As an entrepreneur who, outside of acting, does business consulting and real estate investments, I found myself looking for opportunities to close on legitimate business deals after my stay in Kenya was extended from 2 weeks to a whopping 12 months. I endeavored to approach several businesses with the help of a few connections to make commercials targeted to Americans and other diaspora to come to Kenya to purchase investment properties, to buy and hold, Airbnb, or VRBNB (where people can virtually view potential properties from anywhere in the world from the comfort of their own home). My extensive experience performing in commercials for some of the top companies in the United States has afforded me the opportunity to see how successful projects are executed from the initial casting through production day and into the final marketing ad. So it was to me a no-brainer to use my skillset as an exhorter, actor, and business person to make marketing materials that would be capable of drawing in an American or European audience to be potential buyers in what is known as the fastest growing Urban capital, also seen as the New York of East Africa. To give you an idea of how rapidly Nairobi is growing, the apartment area I lived in, Kilimani, had 4 developments under construction at once, with construction taking place 6 or 7 days a week amid the COVID-19 pandemic. So clearly, there is money still flowing and to be had by the person seeking an opportunity.

There is a story to be told about the attractive woman who endeavors to do business. My first experience was in a gold deal. I was touted as the main broker to broker a deal between a couple of Italian gentlemen; in this case, they weren't interested in doing business with locals, due to the nature of most deals being fraudulent and the lack of honor with locals. So two business acquaintances convinced me to be the trustworthy, nicely dressed American female to basically convince them to buy 265kgs of gold to export out of Kenya. These two Italians openly despised Kenya to me and couldn't care less about its inhabitants; they wanted to make money and leave, returning to their Italian lifestyle, as their disdain for Kenyan food was also evident.

I was sent to a gated community in the Lavington area of Nairobi for the meeting with the two Italian gentlemen. The acquaintance, who was a friend of a friend, picked me up and drove me to the meeting in a Mercedes G-wagon to make things look official. I was greeted at the gate by the guardsman, confirming that I was an expected guest.

The two Italian gentleman waited outside their very posh townhome as I exited the vehicle. They were men of a particular age, in their mid to late 60s. I was escorted into the home, where we sat in the living area, chatting briefly about my background in the States before moving on to the business at hand. Mind you, I have never done a gold deal in my life. These men we clearly not interested in sleeping with me since to me they had a total vibe of a couple. Their affairs were strictly business; however, the one who had sent me to close this deal under the pretense that I was a wealthy American and who had also dropped me off in the high-priced vehicle had mentioned he wanted to marry an additional wife, me. I was promoted by a friend of a friend, since foreigners (the Italians) tend to have little to no trust in Kenyans. I was sent as the pawn of sorts in a deal they figured they couldn't quite pull off without the clout of another foreigner, such as the Italian men trying to complete it. Lesson: don't be a pawn because even if you become a king in the process, the rook may later usurp your King, game over.

The next endeavor was similar to the first in some ways. I went shopping one day at a sports store to find some hiking shoes for my newfound weekend hobby in Kenya. I was dressed for the gym, so I realized that in 2020, not too many people in Kenya wear gym clothes as a leisure outfit, as we do in the States. So it drew a few stares, but nothing I wasn't already used to, being an avid gym goer. As I was browsing the racks for any sportswear that might be on sale, I saw a gentleman watching me out of the corner of my eye. I tried to play it off, but he seemed very intent on observing my every move. I am a very observant individual, and I noticed he was wearing a tailored suit, a pricey-looking button-up shirt, and pristine cuff links. I said nothing and continued to browse. While I walked past his aisle, he said, "You must work out." He patted his belly and said, "I need to get rid of this." Since he was the one who engaged me first, I said yes, I have experience as a personal trainer, amongst other things I do as an entrepreneur, and if he was serious about it, I'd reach out to him. He then began to open his wallet with 2 to 4 inches of cash bulging out to hand me his business card. He says his name is Hermon and his office is near the airport. I took his card, wished him a good day, and continued shopping. He left shortly after, and I didn't think too much into it save for a few clues I picked up on.

Later in the week, I decided to take a chance and give him a call about his other endeavors to see if we could possibly do business in both personal training and other endeavors. He mentioned he would be in town, close to where we had met, so we could grab lunch and discuss everything. I agreed and figured it would be best to put on business attire to shift the focus to bigger opportunities beyond training. I wore a long-sleeve, red, flowy, short-cropped dress and met him at a popular restaurant where people often come to talk business.

As I walked in to meet him, he sat outside in a heavily greened area with lots of grass, plants and palm trees, in yet another handmade suit and a smart dress shirt, dotted with shiny cufflinks. I noticed, but didn't compliment, just to avoid flattering him. We talked about his offices and his cargo business, along with my background in marketing, and how fitness was put on the back burner for me in favor of bigger opportunities in real estate and deal brokering. I excused myself and walked away to wash my hands for the lunch we were about to enjoy. When I came back, he complimented me on my height, my legs, and my attractiveness. I asked how a man of his means lived, whether he was single or married. He told me he was single, after a couple of failed relationships and one child out of the country. He returned the question to me, as I routinely get, so I droned on with the pat answers: single, no kids, never been married. It solicited the *same* response as always, like an actor reciting cliché lines of a script, "Why is a beautiful and intelligent woman like yourself single?" I replied because I haven't met the one yet. After eating a meal of fish and greens, he seemed all too resolute that he had found a partner to do "business" with. He thanked me for meeting with him and invited me to his office to discuss how we can further solidify a business arrangement for brokering gold and other matters, including real estate. I agreed to meet him, and he left me to hurry off to another meeting.

In less than a week's time, we met again in his office, where, true to his description, he had a very plush office suite in the cargo terminal of the Airport. I was invited in by his secretary to wait in a separate lounge as he finished a meeting with another client. After a bit of a wait, the secretary apologized and ushered me into meet Mr. Hermon in an office fit with what looked like a living room filled with posh leather sofas, a 70-inch TV airing the news, and an extra-large mahogany executive desk adorned with small Kenyan flags and a silver-toned statue of a small silver zebra.

I sat on his right-hand side, facing him, in a single-leather chair with two armrests. We began to discuss business, so I tried to take notes in my little red book so I wouldn't miss crucial info on what I thought was a big deal. I then also figured I couldn't write fast enough, so I started taking audio notes to stay in the know. He started mentioning that he wanted to do something bigger than we originally planned, hinting that I could find clients to buy the gold he was storing in his warehouse from businessmen in the Democratic Republic of the Congo. To be honest, I was a bit intrigued. I listened, but had prior knowledge of the negotiations with the Italians under my belt, so I kept one eye open. He continued that we could then split the profits 50/50 because he'd be in charge of releasing the paperwork for export approval, as well as flying the cargo to the desired clientele in Europe or Dubai for refining. The price was discussed, and that's when I dropped my guard because this was an opportunity that didn't come along every day.

We agreed that I would accompany him on a trip to see the groundbreaking for a hotel he was building about two counties away from Nairobi, and to see his other real estate ventures. So I planned to travel with him and his driver to verify the legitimacy of his other business dealings and to get away from the city for a while. In the mid-week early morning, around 6 am, I was greeted at my apartment gate with a freshly detailed black Mercedes (big body, I forget the exact model) 4-door, and the driver swiftly hopped out to take my bags and place them in the trunk so we could be on our way. I was pleasantly surprised because I wasn't even accustomed to this treatment in America. I nestled into the back seat, wrapped myself in a Maasai shuka (a traditional covering that looks like a colorful blanket, often worn by the Maasai tribe in rural areas), and relaxed as we drove to see some new sights.

As we drove, I must admit I felt important and included. We had a short layover after a few hours of driving to have breakfast in Naivasha. There was a medium-sized open-air mall there, with a place called Java cafe, which served breakfast, lunch, and dinner fare, along with gourmet teas and coffee. We ordered and took it to go because at this time, Covid-19 had reached Kenya, and restaurants were not allowing patrons to dine in. We fell back into the vehicle, sipping tea, coffee, and I nibbling on an egg white omelet. We continued on our way to Kisumu, which is very near the center built by Barack Obama in Kogelo.

I was a bit apprehensive about going to an African village. You may ask, "Why?" Well, upon my first week of visiting Kenya, I went to a cultural center that had traditional village homes that were made of mud and clay that people that were over 4 feet tall would have to bend down to get into. They had no heat or flooring. I was conflicted because, culturally, a person could have a lot of wealth and still stick to those traditions without it being unheard of. To my surprise and relief, we pulled up to a gated compound where a young boy, in haste, opened the gate for the boss. There, my eyes saw 6 full houses on a 2.5-acre lot, all very large, made of brick. His house was fitted with a screened porch. As we entered, the driver took my bags and placed them in the home's foyer.

I walked into a nice contemporary bar, a living room with trendy leather sofas and a huge 75-inch flat screen surrounded by speakers. The living area was trimmed with orange touches, along with African art featuring the animals of Nairobi. There was a washer and dryer, which are considered luxury items in Kenya because most either wash by hand or hire a lady to hand wash their clothes for them. This is when Herman took my bag and rolled into his master suite. I noticed this as I checked out which guest room would be best for me to stay in. I quickly walked over to his room while he went back out to the car with the driver, and with an internal laugh, rolled my bag out of his room into the guest room in which I decided upon.

He walked in a caught the tail end of me walking my bag into the guest room and asked, "I thought you were staying in the master suite with me." With his surprise at my action, I retorted, "Uh, no, I'm really fine over here, thanks" (as I held back my laughter). So here is when the intentions were revealed: if he could try his hand early, he would. Later, we convened for a dinner brought by the estate's main servant, as everyone Hermon encountered briskly served him, trying to meet his every demand. We ate a traditional Kenyan meal and later retired for the evening. I cleaned up from our long journey in my private bath adjacent to my guest room, dressed for bed, and began to relax on the bed when I was startled by my door opening. It was Hermon! What did he want? He said, "I thought you might have wanted some company." I said, "Why would you think that, when I chose to be in your guest room?" He asked if I was sure, and I said, "Very!" He bid me goodnight. If memory serves me correctly, I locked the door and went to sleep. The following day, I went to the hotel site and received the plans to build. He expressed concern about a few issues related to structural integrity. I offered to run it by some of my more experienced architects. They later sent documents showing serious flaws in the plans.

Hermon thanked me for getting a second opinion so they could firm up the correct approach. On our last day, I talked to Herman about our friendship and how I was not very trusting of who he was. I felt like he was out to get what he wanted, him being a man of power and all. He assured me that this wasn't the case, just before trying his last attempt to get me to sleep with him. After playfully running away, I realized this was all part of a booty call with a sprinkle of business. I even questioned whether the business was receiving legitimate income. Shortly after returning to the city of Nairobi, I met Hermon again with one of his partners, Simon, from the Democratic Republic of the Congo. He had a very broad accent, but to my surprise was of very light complexion for someone from Sub-Saharan Africa. He spoke with a very thick French accent. We began negotiating the terms for me to broker a gold deal on his behalf. Hermon seemed to play up the fact that he was also interested in me otherwise. Simon insisted the deal would be better if I agreed to be one of his wives. I tried to laugh it off and assure him that as an American woman, I believed in marriage with two people only, but because this was so common ground for men in Kenya to see nothing wrong with adding you to their group, so to speak, I just had to laugh again to lighten things up. The two, Hermon and Simon, stepped away from the table where we had gathered for lunch to meet separately about the terms. Watching their every move, I, being keen, realized that they could also be stepping away to join forces to scheme me into something that would benefit them solely and leave me to hold the proverbial bag.

They returned to the table, joking and laughing as if to suggest they had come to a pass. Both of them sat down briefly to explain that Simon, who had possession of the precious metals in large amounts from his home country, the DRC he wanted me to be a broker to help sell them. We settled that he would give me a price of $38,000 USD per KG, I'd be able to add my price on top of that to make my profit. Hermon said that now that all was settled, he had another meeting to be off to. So he said he would leave, Simon, and me to get acquainted further, discuss any other particulars, and drop me off. In the back of my mind, I feel like there is an "international bro code" that when they left, it wasn't just to discuss business, but to discuss the unsuccessful attempt Hermon had made to sleep with me. So it was as if a proverbial baton were being passed to Simon, who was supposedly wealthy and a power player in the export game.

Shortly after we exchanged a few jokes and finished sipping drinks, he offered me a ride to my destination of home. I walked to his car, and he opened the door to a very well-detailed black Mercedes that was even bigger than the one Hermon and his driver had driven me in. I said thank you and was seated in the front passenger seat. Simon then started entertaining me with sob stories about how he had been taken advantage of in a diamond deal gone bad, where he met with some buyers to show samples. The story rounded out with the folks who were there viewing the sample diamond as a part of a larger parcel, hiring the police to come in and disturb the meeting and confiscating the diamonds, and sending everyone on their way. A sort of group-quick-con where they were able to seize $10,000 to $15,000 USD in diamonds, using the much-underpaid police as an armed enforcer for the endeavor. I listened to his story with some reservations about its validity. He said he must be able to trust me and so on. To me, in retrospect, it was a clever way to play possum and play on a woman's empathy. But I wasn't the one who needed to be auditioned for trustworthiness; it was the other way around.

As we approached the security gate of my flat, he then placed the car in park and asked if he could come inside. I quickly replied, "For what?" You are clearly married in your country, and I am not interested in anything other than business. I furthered, even still, the legitimacy of the business deal has yet to be proven. He encouraged me that in his culture, as a Muslim that having multiple wives was not frowned on but really acceptable. Simon then mentioned that his wife was in another country and that he needed someone who would be close to him here in Nairobi. I think I tried to laugh internally, but it may have spilled out of my mouth in real time. I can't believe this was working on women here. I really had to think for a minute that this culture has extreme poverty, so these outward trappings of success would sway most women over to most anything that they were saying. I politely said I am not interested as a Christian woman in something that does not align with my values, beliefs, and faith. He tried to protest and rebut with the pat answer I've heard from many men of other faiths, that it's ok if they marry outside of their faith. I patted his hand, bid him good evening, and exited the car. I walked to my gate, thinking these guys are really trying it. Is this business or a booty call?

After this experience with his partner, Simon, my trust went from maybe 40% to zero real quick. I began researching more in depth about Hermon, his business, and any articles I could find mentioning anything suspicious. It didn't take long to scroll down to find he had been involved in a gold scam so elaborate that a leader of a very wealthy country fell victim to him. It even had pictures of him in court with one of the guys in the office who had brought me the huge box of gold. It detailed the same account I went through, mentioning being taken to a very posh office, being wooed by him, and having multiple underlings report to him for his every need. Basically, a very thought-out and convincing scam. Hermon and I spoke after I found out all this info, and we scheduled a meeting to complete some paperwork for me to solidify a sale with my buyer in Germany. I planned to continue my visit to his office as if I was none the wiser of his unsavory business deals. The next week, I arrived as scheduled and went through the security protocols to gain entrance to his office, equipped with my trusty laptop.

I was ushered directly into his office, where I was told he would be returning shortly. I quickly cued up my laptop to the articles I found about his involvement in gold scams. He quickly came in, and I had my evidence in place. I stood up to greet him with a hug, which to me was always uncomfortable because he would always try to hug for a bit too long or try to let his hand wander downwards before I would push him away. Back to him, he sat at his very large mahogany desk as if ready to talk about the paperwork we were to complete. I interrupted him to ask if I could show him something. He agreed. I placed my laptop in front of him, and he read and lightly denied the allegations. He pulled up another article on his computer that did not completely exonerate him from the accusation but actually mounted more evidence against him. This story was very public. I closed my laptop, put it back into its black sleeve, and, before exiting his office, said, "I may be beautiful, but I'm not stupid." This ended all my dealings with him and anyone associated with him.

My last experience in Kenya, where business and personal life started to mix, began at the gym with a man I'll call Moe. The gym was part of my daily routine, and in Nairobi, it was more than just a place to work out. It brought together people from different backgrounds, each with their own goals and stories. The air smelled of disinfectant and humidity, with a bit of city dust. The sound of weights and steady music helped me forget about everything outside.

Moe was the kind of man you'd notice even in a crowded room. He was short in stature, but he carried himself with a quiet, magnetic confidence that made him seem larger than life. I noticed him first in one of my abs classes I taught, and then at a boxing sparring session we both participated in—he had the easy charm of someone who belonged everywhere. Every time he came to class, he'd nod at me, a silent acknowledgment that felt like an inside joke.

He always dressed well, even for workouts. His t-shirt was always crisp, his shoes looked new, and his watch caught the light. He had a way of listening closely when you spoke, which made you feel noticed.

One Saturday, the gym hosted a farewell barbecue for someone moving away. The courtyard was full of laughter, the smell of grilled meat, and the friendly atmosphere of people who had worked out together for months. Moe and I sat next to each other, talking about travel, the city, and how to recover from tough workouts. His stories were full of details, and he made every day experiences sound special.

When he asked for my number at the end of the night, it felt natural. Networking, I told myself. In Nairobi, the lines between professional and personal often blurred, and I was used to keeping my guard up. Still, something about Moe piqued my curiosity.

His first message came the next morning. "Great meeting you yesterday. If you ever want to try a new food spot, let me know—I know all the best places." I smiled and replied, "Thanks, will do!" Over the next week, his messages became a gentle background hum: a have-fun text before my morning run, a boxing meme. He was attentive, but never overbearing.

A few days later, Moe invited me to his office. "I have a business proposal, and I'd like your thoughts." He sent the address to a glass tower in Kilimani, a building that showed he was successful. The receptionist greeted me, explained the security steps, and I took the elevator to a floor with a secure door. Moe came out of his office in a tailored suit, smiling.

His office had big windows, dark wood, and cool marble, with views of Nairobi in every direction. He poured tea, told me how he went from tough neighborhoods to working in real estate, and asked about my own journey as we sat on the big balcony overlooking the city. I found myself sharing stories I usually kept private. The way he listened made it feel like he was putting together a puzzle only he could solve.

Then he got to the point: he wanted to sell a big piece of land and needed someone like me to help make the sale. The pay was good, and the chance was exciting. As we talked, our conversation kept drifting—he'd share a childhood memory, ask why I came to Kenya, or tell me about his son.

After that meeting, Moe's presence in my life grew. He'd call in the mornings, send photos from business meetings or coffee shops, and invite me to events. Sometimes he'd send his driver to pick me up in one of his cars, always apologizing if he was running late. Our meetings often ended with lingering conversations about everything and nothing.

The next week, he started inviting me to more business meetings—some with clients, others that felt more like social events. Moe asked if I was busy, and I said I had a meeting set up with his lawyer, whose office was right above on the 8th floor. He seemed glad that I was moving things along quickly to lock in our agreement on the fee for finishing the sale.

I left out and headed up on the elevator to be right on time for our meeting. I walked in, and the receptionist greeted me and then disinfected my hands. She asked me who I had an appointment with, and I mentioned Roy had a scheduled meeting with me in five minutes. She told me to have a seat while she contacted him to confirm. Shortly after, she told me to head back to the office to the far left with the glass doors. As I walked in, Roy stood in the hallway to greet me. I giggled at the fact that he was actually ready for me, since most times Kenyans tended to be late.

He opened the office door and invited me to have a seat. I sat closest to the window, sliding out my laptop to pull up the agreement I had sent him. As I opened the laptop, Roy commented on how well I was doing and complimented the golden details on my computer. I said thanks, but don't let material things impress you into believing things that may not be true. I alluded to this because in Kenya, unless you're driving the latest Range Rover or Mercedes-Benz and have all the latest gadgets, you were deemed unqualified to do business. He chuckled and reiterated, but you are doing well. I said you don't know anything about me, just how I dress, and that my electrical trinkets are new.

I told him clearly that I could sell the land in 45 days if we signed the agreement on my percentage, and if Moe trusted me to show the land to clients and make a marketing presentation for my American developers and investors who could afford a deal this big. Tapping the desk and speaking slowly, I said, "When I set my mind to do something, I get it done"...bro. I'm experienced and have been doing this longer than you. He asked how I could be so sure. I guessed he was younger than me, and I was sure of it. He suggested we make a bet to see if I was right. I was so sure that I said $500 USD, which is 64,000 Kenyan Shillings, says I'm older than you.

I finally saw his ID, and he was my junior by five years, as I suspected from his semi-awkward interactions with me, as if he wasn't fully sure of himself, which is common in younger people. Trying to be nice and not hurt his pockets, I reduced my wager to 3000 Kenyan Shillings, about $30 USD, which I felt was fair for him, doubting my discernment. He said he wasn't going to give me my winnings. "Wow," I said. How am I supposed to trust that, if we reach an agreement on the contract, you and Moe will actually keep your word? "This tells me a lot." He shrugged it off. I further asked, "How can most people who go along with corruption and fail to keep their word complete business in the country successfully?" Semi-regretfully, he said, "That's the way things are done here." I shook my head and said, "That's a sad state of affairs." Before long, we were interrupted by Moe walking in as Roy, and I was laughing hysterically at some silly quip I made about Kenyans. Moe seemed put off by the two of us enjoying ourselves without him. He asked Roy if he had time to go out to lunch with us, and Roy could treat. I laughed and mumbled under my breath that he couldn't treat because he didn't have the money to pay me on the $30 bet he'd lost. Roy talked over me, saying he had things to finish up and couldn't get away. So Moe said we'd head out to lunch and have some of his colleagues meet us there. And we were off.

We went to a nice mall in Nairobi City. The guys who joined us left as quickly as they arrived, saying they had other meetings. So, as usual, it was Moe, his security, and me heading out. Moe dropped me off at my flat and went back to the office to finish business. As I left the car and walked to the doorman who welcomed me back, I couldn't help but notice I was spending almost every day with Moe. It had been quite some time since I spent this much time with a man; it didn't hurt that everywhere we went, he was respected, and that respect was given to me as well. My mind wandered to what it would be like to be with someone I was actually attracted to and loved doing business with. But Moe was taken, or at least that was what Tyra (his co-broker on the land deal) told me, with no clear confirmation from him. I went back to working on my business ideas and proposals. Around this time, I thought it was best to move into a nice studio apartment I had toured earlier.

Tyra and I had planned to meet up at my gym to finish what we couldn't seem to on our first meeting. She agreed to meet me after my spin class. We finally got down to business and hashed out the dates and events we planned to book for a tour group of doctors who were in Kenya to help out with the overloaded hospitals due to the burgeoning Covid-19 crisis, which had suddenly started racking up cases. The doctors were here from Cuba. They were off during the weekend and wanted to enjoy sightseeing and touring around Kenya. So our plan was to make this happen with all the people I had connected with on hiking and touring on my own. I could use these connections, who had proven to do good business, to assist us with our group. Tyra, as always, seemed preoccupied with personal affairs and picked up the phone a few times to deal with her male suitors. I asked if we could get through the agenda planning so I could head out. She agreed, then asked how I was dealing with working with Moe. I said all was fine, to limit distractions from non-work-related matters. Tyra said she had to head out to meet with a friend. I insisted that she sign the JV agreement so I'd know that we were both on the same page. She rushed off to her Uber and said she would email it to me later that evening.

I shook my head in disappointment that the main reason we set up the meeting—to sign off on duties and financial split—was left undone. In disbelief at the continued culture of tardiness and procrastination, I quickly went home. My trust waned completely with Tyra.

I realized that at every business meeting, almost everyone who owned a car or hired a driver had dropped me off at my flat. Knowing this, I felt more at peace knowing that in a week, I'd be moving to a new place where no one would know where I lived. This may seem odd, but in Africa it's not uncommon for a business deal to go bad and for someone to suddenly go missing. Some of the deals were in the multi-million-dollar bracket. I packed a little here and there as the week flew by, with gym sessions and errands. Friday came, and I turned my keys in to the landlord and ordered an Uber to take me to my new place, just a short 10-minute drive away. Now I'd be in the center of every-thing, with a restaurant on the ground floor, a rooftop pool, and an entertainment patio. I was excited for a fresh start, also knowing I'd be leaving soon to head back to the United States.

Weeks turned into over a month, and I still had not received a signed agreement from Moe for my payment on his property in Maasai Mara, or for me taking the lead on the sale. I called and texted his lawyer many times, but no response. His lawyer finally said my fee was too high for him. I quickly changed the fee and waited for his answer, but nothing happened. Moe's lawyer seemed to be wasting time, so I decided not to go to any more meetings or talk further unless it was about signing the agreement for my work. After changing my fee to the usual international rate, I asked Roy to tell him right away because I wasn't going to wait any longer to be ignored. I didn't really trust Roy to follow through; he worked for Moe and had to do what Moe said.

I decided in my mind to go to the Mara because this was a trip I wanted to take anyway, and after returning, I would not show up for any additional meetings with clients until Moe and I had a one-on-one talk about him agreeing to sign, or, as an alternative, me walking away.

We had a meeting set up to take the client to see the land in less than a week. I arranged for a camera crew to come along so we could save time and money by filming the land and its features to make a video for other serious buyers. This way, we wouldn't have to take everyone on a full-day safari, which is expensive and usually paid for by the owner, just to convince the client to make a quick decision. The camera crew had to work with a very small budget to get footage that would normally take two days, but now had to fit it into half a day. We confirmed them, and I set up their transport with their gear. I felt uneasy because Tyra would be coming, and she had completely disappeared, not answering my calls, texts, or voicemails about the partnership. We had met several times to plan, and I had spent hours writing the contract to spell out our duties. She hadn't replied in the three weeks since I last saw her at the gym for our planning session. I wondered if something bad had happened to her because of her relationships with some of her boyfriends. Did she get into a fight? Were her children hurt? Did she decide to do the business alone? Did she go back to Moe and tell him what I really thought about him outside of business? All these thoughts ran through my mind.

We all received a text confirmation that we would meet up at dusk at a nearby fueling station/breakfast hub to board the Safari truck. The camera crew would follow us to a midway point, where a second safari truck would serve as our mode of transport to the land parcel. The cameras would start filming footage before we reached the land as a lead-up, B-roll, building anticipation for the potential buyer by showing the surrounding areas, including numerous wild animals in their natural environment. All parties agreed through confirmation via text message. I went to bed early to be ready the following morning for all the emotions and acting I had to do. How would I interact with a so-called business partner who has practically avoided speaking with me about the contract or terms?

What would my encounter be like with Tyra? Who has managed to ignore my attempts to reach out to her and now I know that she is physically alright because she confirmed her attendance to accompany us on this trip to see the land with a client that neither she nor I had brought to the table; but rather a third party that I had been previously introduced to in prior meetings where Tyra was not present. I prepared myself with prayer and confirmation that I had not changed who I was since the beginning of my encounters with Moe and Tyra. My actions closely followed my verbal conversations; integrity is important to me, and my patience was tested by both. My goal was to be the same fun, focused, and fearless businessperson who attracted these two to want to include me in the first place, sans the naïveté of how people respond when making money is the goal. The rose-colored glasses were off, and the self-assured, observant student of behavior showed up with God on my side.

The morning came, and I hustled to get ready for an exciting day of seeing parts of Kenya I had not traversed, which was motivation in itself. My backpack was ready with extra chargers, headphones, a journal, a laptop, and essentials. Uber ready, I trotted off, not wanting to be the last one to show up at the rendezvous point. I had no expectations other than that the camera crew would deliver as promised. Admittedly, I was a bit nervous to see Moe, as attraction, unanswered questions, and power struggles can make anyone uneasy. However, I wanted to see this through, even if the end of the road was literally the visit to see the land. I had resolved that one thing in my mind: there is strength in being willing to walk away from something completely if the rules of play are broken.

I popped out of the Uber with just a hint of daylight cracking the sky, and the air a bit chilly. I greeted the client, his broker, and Moe's security, who had made it before me. I saw the safari truck waiting trustily by for our full party to arrive. We were still missing the two people, along with the camera crew, who posed the most questions about how this trip would actually turn out: Tyra and Moe. The fellas and I went to have some light breakfast/ tea until the others arrived. I ran to grab a few snacks from the convenience store before sitting to have tea with Moe's security. A call came to his phone; it was none other than his boss, Moe.

He had arrived and wanted us to board the truck and prepare to leave. Loading up my backpack, phone, and snacks, I walked to the safari truck, not knowing what to expect. First, in sight was Tyra sitting in the truck. Catching a glimpse of her while I instructed the camera crew to follow behind us to a midway point, where they would switch off and board a separate truck to house their equipment. The next hurdle was to see Moe, while navigating where I should sit in all this internal confusion, mentally taking a deep breath. I hopped in, claiming my spot at the front just next to Moe's backpack.

I greeted Tyra and asked what happened to her being as though I hadn't heard from her since our meeting at the gym. "Girl, I didn't know if you were still alive with all that drama you told me about." "I left you several messages to see if you were ok, and to get a corresponding signature on the contract for the work you wanted to do." Tyra gave a bit of a bland excuse for completely disappearing for 3 weeks. I was over it and resolved not to have any further meetings or business with her from this point on; however, I remained cordial, pleasant, upbeat, and humorous to keep my demeanor lighthearted despite the incongruencies of these relationships. Shortly thereafter, a happy-go-lucky Moe pops up to the truck. I smile and greet him, trying to hide the awkwardness between us over his refusal to sign the contract, so I can continue working as a broker on the deal to sell the land.

Even though I was calm, talkative, and smiling, I put on my headphones and wrote on my laptop to pass the time and keep myself from talking too much. As soon as I took off my headphones, Moe made me the DJ and asked me to use my phone to play music on a Bluetooth speaker he brought, since the truck didn't have any new music hookups. I agreed, giving up my quiet ride to play music for everyone.

I joked a lot and laughed often to relieve the uneasiness until shortly after I forgot all about the interworking of what did and did not happen within the group. After a couple of hours, Moe said we would stop for breakfast. We stopped at what seemed like a popular café where a large group of very international-looking gentlemen were celebrating a birthday. We crowded around a couple of tables, and Tyra ventured to sit next to me. She seemed to resume her girlfriend-like status after my light reprimand of her behavior at the beginning of our trip. Tugging my arm as Moe walked off in the distance to make a phone call, Tyra said, girl, let me tell you what happened with the doctor and me. This was the guy we had met at his house on my first introduction to Tyra, the one Moe and I both presumed she had a relationship with.

She said he had gotten a bit vindictive, refusing to pay for things they had agreed on. She helped him furnish his newly purchased home. After an unfriendly split between the two, he had made a so-called running tab of the things he did for her and purchased as a married man having an affair. That he wasn't willing to pay for her services to interior decorate his home because the relationship had dissolved, so he said the items he purchased for her, offset the items she purchased for the home.

My eyes rolled, "What would you expect from someone shady enough to cheat?" "No one here seems to keep their word about anything", I mentioned. She was angry. I said he's not so smart to start a battle when you know where he lives, and you told me his wife would actually be arriving soon from the United States to live in the home with him. Tyra said she wanted to come back to collect the items she wasn't paid for. I advised her that counting it as a loss and moving on would be the better choice. This made the group dynamic even odder; she hadn't told Moe that the internal battle between the two of them was brewing. Dr.Verlund was supposed to be one of the primary clients, along with a group of other doctors, to consider purchasing the land to develop a hotel or several boutique villas. This was beyond messy, and I was so happy that I tried to maintain my professionalism by not getting involved in dating or business. Tyra brought her conversation to an abrupt close as Moe approached the table to rejoin us, since the breakfast had arrived. We both sprang out laughing because of the sad lives these guys led, trying to hide their indiscretions, business, and personal lives. I must say, I much preferred having a life where I wasn't being juggled by multiple men who were only 2 or 3 degrees of separation away. God was giving me an opportunity to see that when we think the grass is greener on the other side of the world, it isn't when it comes to fidelity and relationships.

We finished our meal and pulled out as a group to meet the second safari van to get the cameramen to make the switch. The day went on, and we enjoyed a brunch at a nearby resort in Naserian Mara before heading out to see the land. As we loaded back in the truck, we went off-road through the grass and wild animals I had never seen before, then some familiar suspects, zebras and baboons. We abruptly stopped at a piece of land next to the Mara River and observed eight to ten hippos cooling off in the river. Our Maasai guide told us that we must watch the time carefully because, a little after dusk, the hippos would come out and enter the land we were standing on to dry off and rest for the evening.

The cameraman buzzed his drone to and fro over the property while Moe gave the potential buyer a rundown of the land. It seems that just as quickly as we arrived, we headed out into the sunset with a landscape of giraffes and buffalo alongside us. After several long hours of driving, we finally made it back to Nairobi. We were breaking curfew at this point because it was almost midnight, and the county curfew was 9pm East African time due to the COVID pandemic, which aimed to reduce public mingling. The safari truck dropped each one of us at our destinations, and I chose to be dropped off a few blocks away from where I lived. My trust was at zero at this point, given all the broken promises, and I didn't trust anyone enough to let them know where I lived. As I crossed the main intersection, a large truck stopped me and began speaking fluent Swahili. After a moment or two, I realized they were the police. I continued speaking in English, hoping this would deter them from any wrongdoing. I relied on my American accent to get me out of this jam. The officers switched to English and said I was under arrest as I saw multiple guns, G3s, and AK-47s slung over their shoulders. I said no, I AM NOT, I'm going to cross the street and go home. They insisted that I get into the back of the truck's tented area. I confidently retorted, "I am going to walk across this street and go to my apartment." Mind you, I was still at least three blocks away from my place. They gave up and said, "Go immediately," so I did. After speed walking home, I was satisfied that I had enough excitement to last me a few days. As I entered my apartment foyer near the front desk, I noticed I had missed calls from Tyra, asking if I was alright and if I had made it home safely. I briefly informed her that I had been detained by the police for a short while but made it home without a hitch. She seemed a bit hysterical, asking why I didn't allow the driver to drop me directly in front of my gate. I knew the answer (to keep these untrustworthy people from knowing where I lived), but I remained quiet and said it didn't matter, because I was here now.

There was a subsequent follow-up call from Moe asking me if I was alright. I guess the word traveled fast that I was stopped by the police. He asked me if I was alright and repeated the same question Tyra had, regarding why I didn't let the truck drop me off in front of my place. I told him I didn't want them to have to go out that way when they had others to drop off after me. So, instead, they dropped me off at the closest main road so they could continue their journey, as it was well past curfew for them as well. He reprimanded me a bit for being so stubborn. I received the rebukes, said everything worked out, so it wasn't so bad, and bade him adieu so I could get some rest after all the excitement of the day.

The week had begun, and I had started my strategy to get the contract signed or walk away from the "deal" to sell the property. I planned to give him 4 days to respond before waking early and waiting for him at his office for an impromptu meeting to get an answer. Moe never reached back out to me after the call regarding the police stopping me on the street. So, faithful to myself, I executed my plan, like clockwork, during the mid-week. I rose early, prepared my best-looking business casual dress, and reviewed my notes from a book I was reading at the time called the '1 Minute Negotiator' by Don Hutson and George Lucas, showing up unannounced to his highly secured office. I believe God was on my side in getting to the bottom of things, because I had been to his office before and security let me in with no questions asked. Security at the building's perimeter greeted me when I exited my Uber, then security at the front desk, which checks ID and issues a permission ticket to access the building, checked me in as usual, with all the pleasantries. The next step would be very hard: either gaining entry to the office, which requires fingerprint access only, or communicating through the call box to his secretary, who only allows visitors with an appointment. Just as I thought of this, his chauffeur arrived on the ground floor to greet me, and he escorted me up to the office on the 7th floor and opened the door for me. He directs me to the conference room to wait for Moe to arrive. Now you know: this had to be God, because I managed to evade every last security measure to make it into his office, totally free and clear.

As I waited, I opened my notebook and reviewed the key points I wanted to convey. Mainly, his avoidance strategy, which the book says is no strategy at all but more of a form of procrastination, delaying a decision. Moe was what the book called a negotia-phobe. His fear of making a decision that would be collaborative, meaning a win-win for both parties, had him stuck in not making a decision at all. He arrived. I was in earshot as he was told I was waiting for him. I sensed his surprise, as he came in to tell me I could come into his office to talk.

I got up, packed my book and phone, which I was continuing to listen to an audiobook on, as I waited. I trapesed ever so casually into his office and sat. He offered me some tea while inviting me to sit on the balcony of his office, which overlooked Nairobi. We sat, and he mentioned how impressed he was at the initiative I took to come and meet with him. Moe mentioned that my timing was perfect because at this time, he normally doesn't set any appointments but reads the paper and prepares his mind for the day. Remaining calm in my demeanor, I tried to get to the bottom of what was unspoken between us. I softly said after taking a sip of my tea, "Please tell me what's going on, and I mean in every way, business and personal."

Moe was very intentional with every word he spoke. I had never seen him choose each word oh so carefully before he uttered them. He initiated the talk by reviewing how we met at the gym. He was so curious about who I was. This American girl who could box in the ring during a sparring session with semi-pro guys, this girl who I saw coming to events after the gym where we sat and ate with friends, drank and socialized, this woman who, when she showed up, everyone seemed to acknowledge her presence in the business meeting I invited her to. This woman, whom I spent the entire day with, went from meeting to meeting, introducing her to my colleagues, business associates, and friends. I interjected ever so carefully, "Moe, where are you going with all of this?" He said I like you, Mia. I found myself liking you a lot. The more time I spent with you, the more I realized that we worked well together. That's when I proposed that you help me take over some of my other business ventures to liquidate, so I could focus solely on my main company. I was reluctant to tell you my situation because I truly had feelings for you. I live with someone, and we are together, and of course you know about my son. So I said you were totally unavailable to me, but you acted like you were, rather than being forthcoming from the moment you knew me. He apologized and said, "Mia, it's not easy for a man like myself to admit that." He continued on to ask me if I was attracted to him, and I said that it really didn't matter since he was physically in a relationship with a person I would consider to be his wife, if they were living together, and he was emotionally unavailable as a result of the former reasoning, regardless of the problems that we might have faced in the past. As he mentioned, she had moved out and into a separate home for some time and quite recently moved back. This, in fact, was none of my business and was out of the scope of what I was here to do with him, which was to broker a deal on his behalf.

We continued. I asked him why he didn't sign the contract after all the effort I put into drafting it, revising it to acceptable terms, and meeting with his lawyer several times to see if it met his approval. He started by saying he intended to follow through, but made promises to other brokers prematurely, which put him in an awkward position that forced him to reduce the agreed-upon fees to a lower percentage or remove a broker altogether if they were unable to produce a client. I mentioned to him that this wasn't what we discussed. I informed him that your personal feelings, lack of communication, and fear of negotiation have landed you in this situation. I mentioned to him that I wouldn't have minded it so much if the percentage profit had been reduced, as long as you had clearly communicated to me when things changed. However, to me, it seemed as if you were playing a bit of a game to see if I would keep showing up and using my status as a good-looking American broker, without an agreement on my fees, to talk with potential clients.

This was a mess and a clear lesson: the thin line between a man wanting a secret relationship and making a real business deal was his biggest struggle. Later that week, I gave back a bag of a few souvenirs he gave me, a red Kenya hat, and a couple of other small things through his personal trainer and deleted his number. That's when things got ugly. He sent angry emails demanding the video footage from the Mara, which I didn't have, but the cameraman did and hadn't been paid for. Again, he wanted things he hadn't paid for and was demanding before paying the bill. I contacted the cameraman and told him Moe's office wanted him to come in to get the check so he could send the files. He did, confirmed he got paid, and sent me the files. The files were huge and took about a day to download because the internet in Nairobi, especially in my apartment, was slow. In one day, I got mean email threads from his employees and coworkers saying I was never worth doing business with, and that Moe's choice to work with me was a big mistake. I laughed it off and sent him the files. I was supposed to do the voiceover for the video, but I didn't want to do any more business with him. He asked my rates before I sent the files, and after his angry emails, because he couldn't get what he wanted from me for free in business or in his personal life, he tried to make me look bad to his coworkers, who I felt knew about his mistakes but had to take his side to keep their jobs. I moved on quickly, seeing it as a big lesson as a woman doing business in a male-dominated society in Africa. High corruption and low morals have made this modern-day Wild West a tough place for women to do business, with no side of booty call.

I later booked my ticket back to the United States, as this was the nail in the coffin for me. Of multiple business deals, only a small venture granting a microloan to a young Kenyan entrepreneur was successful. There were many positives: I made dozens of connections for future business and friendships that proved invaluable. I was mentally over it. I felt I was successful in learning the fundamentals of business and most interpersonal relationships in Kenya. There must be a clear line between business and personal interests, including romantic relationships. If these lines are blurred, it opens the door to confusion. The delicate balance of being a positive, kind-hearted, easy-going woman in business while also presenting as professional, matter-of-fact, and no-nonsense is a game that seems hard-won. Present yourself as an attractive catch, say what you mean and mean what you say, but don't be willing to be a booty call for a man who has no real interest in doing business with you. If you draw a hard line, you might be disliked, but you will always be respected as a woman who was not willing to go morally bankrupt in pursuit of your bottom line.

Chapter 19

Too Many Chances

As Christians, we are called to forgive and live at peace with others as far as it depends on us as individuals (Romans 12:18). As women who have not been embittered by the many bad experiences in life, relationships, and business, there tends to be a soft spot within most of us to overlook bad behavior or character. Speaking for myself, I tended to disregard the old adage by Maya Angelou that says, "If someone shows you who they are, believe them the first time." Despite those words of wisdom, I will take you through a scenario in which I have learned this valuable lesson the hard way. Perhaps we can all put this into practice, Lord willing, moving forward.

Being on social media sometimes feels like a requirement for my profession; every so often, I post a pic or video to market myself and secure future work. At one point in my life, maybe 8 to 9 years ago, I wore my hair in a natural afro style most of the time, and I was very introverted unless I was throwing an event or meeting with clients for my fitness business. One day, after posting some pics I took with a friend, who is a photographer with a very nice studio in Howard County, Maryland. I received the usual well-wishes, likes, and comments from friends and acquaintances. One thing that particularly stood out was a DM (direct message) or PM (private message) from a guy I didn't really know. Being curious, as most would be, I checked out his page and found other pictures of him and his business. He always seemed well overdone, with his hair and facial hair, reminding me of something out of early 1920s mobster movies. I honestly didn't know what to think. The message read, "I think you seem to be a nice person and I would like to talk or meet up sometime, to show you my establishment." Honestly, I was kinda intrigued, thinking to myself, of all the people on the internet, why did you single me out and contact me? I was a bit suspicious right away because, from the pic he liked, I definitely didn't seem like his type. At that time, I felt I was a bit plain; I wasn't overly showy in my style of dress, not bad, but surely not the highest of caliber, which I'm pretty sure he'd preferred.

I responded, "Hello, I got your message and here is my number, feel free to call so we can chat sometime." I believe he responded after a few days, saying "ok." Later that week, I received a call in the evening, around 7pm or 8 pm, from a number I hadn't seen before but that looked local to the area. I cautiously picked up, not mentioning my name, just saying hello. He said hi and mentioned our message on Facebook. So, after realizing it was him, I greeted him and began getting to know each other. He immediately began talking about his business endeavors, how he built it through hard work, and how he had multiple locations. I felt like he started rambling on a bit. So I don't know what told me to do this, but I took my phone and found the timer, and started it. I soon realized, after we exchanged greetings, that he completely took over the conversation with a monologue about himself, lasting, according to my phone, nearly 20 minutes nonstop. He droned on about how great his business was doing and all the work that went into making it a success.

Please don't get me wrong, I love supporting business owners, most of my friends and acquaintances know that if I have the opportunity to support them, I will, first and foremost. So in my heart, I was not in any way jealous; I was actually happy for him. However, I wanted to have a conversation where we could both get to know each other through an even exchange of dialogue. Time pressed on, I looked at my phone, and it had now been twenty-five minutes straight, and there was hardly any attempt to ask me questions or get to know anything about me. I became frustrated at this one-sided experience and made some excuse to get off the phone. I was exhausted from a conversation with a man, possibly a couple of decades my senior, who didn't have the etiquette to even inquire about the woman he "he said" he was interested in, according to the original Facebook message. I told him it had been a long day and I had some other things to get done before I turned in for bed. He mentioned he was still at work and he had a late-night meeting with his employees, so we bid each other good night.

Drained from the conversation, I was astounded that someone could be so self-absorbed. He texted me on and off throughout the month, saying he was throwing a big holiday party and wanted me to come, and that I could bring a friend. Honestly, I was a bit excited to attend because during the winter months, there aren't as many social events. My home, gym, work, church, and grocery store routine was becoming so mundane. I wanted an opportunity to meet some cool people, network, laugh, talk, and socialize. He sent me a digital flyer from a previous event, along with a link to photos and video taken by the event photographer.

I scrolled through, looking at the venue's preview and the flashes of cars pulling up for valet parking. The outfits, the smiles of the attendees as they took pics with him, and the host and their friends. The shots of the dance floor with bright strobe lights and the DJ chanting to the crowd. It looked very interesting, the place to be for all the "who's who" of the area. I looked at the pics and thought to myself, "Do I even fit in with this crowd?"

Regardless of whether I did or not, I just wanted to go with a home girl of mine, laugh, enjoy, and have fun for a change, instead of the constant hustle. I reached out to my friend and told her about the event, forwarding the same links and a few pictures so she could get an idea of how to dress if she was really interested in going. She thought it would be fun and was game to come along. A couple of weeks passed, and the party date came and went. I thought he said he'd send me the invitation so I could make plans to go. This was a huge red flag. Why would someone tell me about a party and send an invite.

To me, this was a bit of a bad way to start getting to know someone. It felt like it was a show-off tactic. I will show you what I'm doing and not invite you, a classic game of showing dominance or superiority, to leave the wanting prey on the outside as a bystander. I overlooked the offense, but I can't say it didn't disturb my spirit, or I wouldn't be writing about it. So we continued chatting until things eventually turned into just talk and never meeting up. Eventually, our talks and texts died off, only to resume a couple of years later, when I asked why he hadn't bothered to set a time and place to meet. He made all kinds of excuses about his schedule, crazy work hours, and, I felt, that our meeting was not high on his priority list.

This time around, he seemed more interested in getting to know at least a few things about me. It wasn't too far down this track that this inquisition became sexual in nature. After several minutes of him explaining why he's still single, due to sexual incompatibility with his female counterparts. He proceeded to ask me about what I preferred sexually and was redirected several times. I was now referred to as sex-a-phobic, from a man that I never met in person and who still didn't know much about who I was as a person. I rebutted that knowing someone in a sexual manner was probably the least important on the list, comparable to character, being trustworthy, similar thoughts on religious belief, mutual attraction, and overall chemistry.

He was adamant in his mind's eye that the key to failure in his relationships was mostly sexual and a lack of initiation (on her part) of interesting conversation. I thought, poor communication of the issues in the relationship, lack of patience, and overstressing the importance of knowing how to do sexual favors to his exact liking might be the bigger issue. His rebuttal was that it was important to him. I thought if that was his priority, who was I to change it? However, I could only share my perspective. We chatted sporadically throughout the weeks, and at one point, it became consistent. I reached out to him for advice on voiceover auditions and which one he thought sounded best, as a business owner with expert experience in marketing. Calls became more frequent, and sometimes we'd chat about all things serious or nothing at all. There was an underlying need sometimes for him to shift the conversation sideways for phone sex, in which I declined, and most times didn't want an argument with the name-calling of me being a sex-a-phoebe to a guy I still haven't met and am not even in a committed relationship with. The question still remained: when would there be a chance for us to meet up?

It was almost the end of summer, and I was invited to a red carpet for a web series in which I had a small role. I remember it was a very busy day; I was on a panel for actor advisement earlier that day in Maryland. I planned to go from one event to the other. I had to travel from Baltimore to DC, so I brought my clothes and planned to shower and change at one of my gym affiliates. Today, it crossed my mind to reach out to him because I remember him mentioning that his office was not far from where I'd be passing on my way to the event in DC. I called his phone, and, as usual, he picked up. He said "What are you up to"? I told him I was on the way to an event, but I had a bit of time before it started. He told me to stop by his office so we could finally catch up. So, I said Why not. It wasn't that far from where I was, so I rerouted my GPS and headed his way.

I pulled up into the parking lot and got out of the car. I took my change of clothes with me because I thought, maybe, if time got too short, I'd change at his office and leave from there for the red carpet event, which was about 30 minutes away. He greeted me at the door in a bit of a hurry, saying that he was going to hop in the shower and come back out, and I could make myself comfortable until then. His office was very sprawling, with multiple rooms, a gym, a few offices, and a large living room-like area with flat screen TVs. I came in and made myself comfortable, waiting to have a conversation to get to know each other. It took almost an hour and a half for him to shower and get dressed, so I was really annoyed that I was invited to an office to sit by myself and not be engaged with the person I came to see.

I was on the fence, so much time had passed that I wasn't sure if I still wanted to go to the event, and by now, I was extremely hungry. He finally came out of his personal bathroom to greet me and chat. I said, "Wow, it sure took you a long time to come out and greet me." I would have thought you would already be dressed by this time of day. He apologized and said he had been up very late working. I mentioned my event and that I was running late because I was waiting for him. I told him I wasn't sure if I'd be able to make it in time. I mentioned that now I was extremely hungry because I had been on the go all day. He offered to take me out to eat. So I agreed, not knowing that we still wouldn't go right away. At this point, I wasn't going to make the event and was super moody from not eating all day, since I'd come from a seminar and was one of the panelists earlier that morning. He then said to leave my car there at this office, and we would go in his car to the...BARBERSHOP?

He couldn't be serious?! After coming in, sitting alone and watching TV, waiting for him to shower and change, which took over an hour, NOW we are going for a haircut?!! All this to go grab a quick bite? I was immediately exhausted. How could I be in a relationship with someone who takes longer to get ready than a woman does?

So off to the barber we went. We drove to the first shop that was closed, then to a second, and we had to negotiate to get him a haircut because they were about to close as well. I sat inside and waited for his cut to be finished, talking about the patience of Job. This was another hour-and-a-half process. So I'm about 3 hours into my visit to his office, and we still haven't engaged much because it's been all about him grooming himself, SIGH. He promised to make it up to me by taking me to a really nice seafood restaurant. I agreed because I was extra hungry and wanted something really good to eat. And I was not disappointed. He pulled up to valet the car, and we went into one of the nicer restaurants featuring market-priced seafood. They seemed to already know him there, and they sat us right away in a large booth near the front.

He asked me what I like to drink, and I told him I don't drink anything but tea and sparkling water. He ordered a fancy-colored liquor beverage and asked me to taste it; I discreetly declined. We enjoyed eating dinner and felt like the evening went pretty well after it FINALLY got started. I really tried hard to be modest with my food ordering, because I really don't like overeating when I'm on track with the gym and doing well with portion control. So, as he insisted, we ordered a double serving of seafood after I suggested we share a single plate. The food was delicious, and I felt it was well worth the wait. We left, and he drove me back to his office to end a very long day. He invited me to stay back and chill with him. I politely declined because this wasn't the hour of night "just to chill". I politely thanked him for dinner and made my way back to Baltimore.

At this point, I convinced myself that I should give him a chance, just be friends, and see, despite my being super skeptical of him. And after talking for a while, just like clockwork, it was good for a while, him being available to talk to me, but me always having to make an effort to go see him. He kept asking when I would be in the area. That area is 45 minutes from where I resided. My thoughts were, "Why do I have to go out of my way to see a person who said they were interested in me?" I was super annoyed by this because, if it hadn't been for my coming to see him at his office, we would never have met in person. As our conversation progressed, I guessed he sensed my frustration and planned to come to Baltimore to take me to an event.

He said his friend from a mutual college was having a birthday celebration, to be held at a large venue in Baltimore. I agreed to accompany him even though I didn't think I had anything fancy enough to wear, so I wore black that matched his attire. Nonetheless, I felt it was an effort on his part to finally come to me, despite his busy schedule. So we attended the event, and I bumped into some folks who knew me from my childhood. The event was cool, but I felt a bit out of place because I was considerably younger than most there, so there wasn't much to chat about with the folks at the table. It was good, however, when I got up to move around to chat with the folks who had known me most of my adolescence. He caught up with other buddies, and we soon left to get, according to him, "some better food options". This was a bit weird because we were served food (a whole dinner, to be exact) at the event. This was another red flag. A person who can't control their appetite is a cautionary tale of other things within themselves they can't control. To me, it was a bit ridiculous to eat twice in less than an hour.

To sum it up, this became one of those roller coasters where we talked consistently, then went through a long period of disappearances. I felt, and knew in my heart of hearts, that this was common with him, as my discernment told me he was a player who didn't share the same values I did. Especially since he was almost 2 decades my senior, had never had kids, and had never been married.

He and my gut literally told me he is enjoying women, like par for the course, a part of being well off. Like no one blinks an eye at these things. These types of men will try to convince you that the reason they haven't settled down is that they haven't found their sexual match. After willfully volunteering info about enjoying multiple sexual partners at one time without even a stutter, I really started to think, is this all that is out here? No matter where you go as a woman, the church, the street, or the workplace, there only seems to be the man who cares nothing about starting a whole family unit or maintaining one without infidelity. I understand single men are not obligated to anyone, but I just thought, "What is the entire purpose of amassing wealth that only less than 1% of the entire world has, if you don't have anyone to love or to leave it to via your legacy?" This was a miserable endeavor, to say the least. Furthermore, "What would it profit a man to gain the whole world and lose his soul"22This guy had a lot, but seemed so unhappy to me. Imagine having to continuously hunt for things or people to give you a temporary thrill, a high of sorts, and when you achieve that additional business to open or sleep with that woman you have been pinning away for, the high fades. You become a bit depressed because "it", "The High," never lasts.

Regardless of all this, I cycled back into the train wreck of a situation, thinking I could be different and show him God, a true relationship with Christ, and settling down to start a family might be a joy he could attain, if he decided to stop running away and to the idol of success. I entered into this rigged attempt for yet another try. We ran into each other a couple of years after our last meeting. I attended a party at a mutual friend's house, and he was there. It did cross my mind that he might come, but I also thought he might not, given how obsessed he was with work. So I may have some peace to enjoy myself unbothered. NOPE. As my intuition told me. He arrives in grand fashion with what looks like an older lady friend and his usual flashy attire (mental sigh). I prepared myself. I was in a great conversation while this was taking place, regarding the movie industry and relationships; the patio was buzzing. He struggled to visually gain my attention. I finished my conversation, went into the house, and was greeted by another acquaintance, who I hung out with once a blue moon, in the married and thirsty category. What I mean is that a man who chose to be married but is unhappy and lives his life as if he were single. He wanted to engage me in pointless conversation so he can almost mark his territory to a degree and show me he is still interested. I tried to politely engage in this go-nowhere exchange, and I did. As we were talking, the guy I dated on and off intentionally cut through our conversation, since we were both standing a few feet apart. He must, like a peacock, strut through to let me know he is here and wants to speak to me when I have time.

I did my best to enjoy the function as if he were not there, but each time I engaged with someone, he seemed to hover to gain my attention. Eventually, I just stopped and talked with him before leaving. My soul told me not much had changed, but my heart was none the wiser. After our conversation about him convincing me to give it another chance and him immediately discarding the friend he'd come with to leave with me, I knew this wasn't what I'd hoped, but my heart really did hope that, with time, things would change.

Upon arrival at his place, it was like we went right back into the same old routine of him ignoring me unless he was pandering for sex. I felt empty. I just went into another room to pray and cry myself to sleep. What stung more than anything was seeing, in the room I chose to sleep in, a card I had handwritten a few years prior, congratulating him on his accomplishments and new home, set at attention on the dresser. There was an aside written, asking if he'd see the house filled with a loving family one day. I'd be interested in working with him to achieve it. This made me cry even more because I really thought he might have wanted that same thing, him cherishing the card for so many years and placing it on his mantle as a reminder.

Scrolling my mind down memory lane, our encounters seemed sprinkled with a tug-of-war. A battle, so to speak, of him wanting to keep achieving more and more without the same effort being put into a healthy relationship, spiritual maturity in learning the word of God, and making physical health a priority. I also remembered good times of play-fighting and trash-talking, great get-togethers with his friends or family, and watching movies together at the theater. These are the things I desired more than all the material things he was more than capable of offering me with ease. My soul felt there was a huge disconnect in our values, and later, the obsession with wanting to make me sin, told me that absolutely nothing had changed but my level of compromise, what I truly desired in a relationship: love, not lust, and dedication to be followers of Christ together above all. The fullest realization of circumstances enveloped me in a state of numbness. That all the money, cars, big houses will never fulfill my need for a man who could earnestly pray for me, not prey on me.

Maybe he genuinely wanted the same as me, or maybe not. That's only for God to judge. Regardless, the fact of the matter is this: if the person is not willing to put in the work to become the person God wants them to be, individually or in a relationship that leads to marriage, there is no number of chances that will change who they are at their core. No amount of chances can make someone value understanding what it means to be a biblically defined husband. The church has pounded into the minds of women what the definition of a Proverbs 31 woman is, but has woefully failed to show men the characteristics of Proverbs 31 and Ephesians 5 man.

Our responsibility as Godly women is to forgive, but not to keep giving too many chances for someone to abuse the opportunities we give them. If someone is not producing the fruits of change, they will be like the fig tree that Jesus cursed in Matthew 21:18-22; they look good with green leaves, but are woefully barren (knowledge of the word), evoking no obedience to Christ in their actions.

Chapter 20
Still Single...Now What?

In this modern world, we can get caught up in online battles between men and women. The Red pill vs. feminism and so on. The thought that something must be wrong with you if you don't have a boyfriend or husband is absurd when women have been told by the collective to choose better. So we have! If you are in a committed relationship, you are technically considered single until you are married, and my hope is that the relationship is thriving and that the blessing of marriage is soon on your horizon. If you are not in a committed relationship and are navigating "these single streets." It's also my prayer that if it is your desire for a marriage to a suitable mate, that you would receive it as well. Being single, no matter in a relationship, dating to find the one, or completely out of the market, healing and doing the self-work it takes to be the best you can be. We, as women, must take note that it *might not* happen. Or it won't happen when you think it should. Then what?

I have written down things I felt God wanted me to do and have put some off for years, or have slowly tried to finish them to no avail. This book was one of those endeavors. There is a purpose to your life in the meantime of the waiting season that needs you to fulfill those tasks God has whispered in your ear to complete. Maybe God is telling you to finish your book, to work on building a closer relationship with God by finding a church, attending bible study regularly, maybe to travel to teach in another country, go back to school for that degree, volunteer to teach at your church or community center, possibly committing this year to getting your health and fitness on track once and for all, learning a trade to understand home renovations, or going to therapy, grief counseling, maybe starting that business. Whatever it is that has been on the table of your heart but has been left undone because of the distractions of relationships, must be completed.

This is our season, not to abandon ourselves or our visions, but to use this time wisely to put our hand to the plow of life and not turn back until we have kept our promises to ourselves. God wants us to live an abundant life, but that life will not be free of problems. It will be one where your relationship with him will be so close that you will see how great he can be walking alongside you in this season and the next.

This book was a journey for me to be obedient, no matter how small the step and novice the attempt. Even though I have tried to remain faithful, I have made mistakes and stumbled along the way. Said things that wasn't representative of the woman I want to be in God's eyes and done things I thought I was delivered from. Now what? You and I have been forgiven if we have asked in prayer. This is a new beginning. The past is over! Let's walk by faith to complete what God has placed us on this earth to achieve for his glory. Let's get to work being the woman God wants us to be, with the dreams he has placed inside of us. Let's get to work just like Ruth in the field, and our hands will be so busy that we won't notice the time passing until God sends the man that is destined to be our mate, and if that doesn't happen, we know we have done the work God called us to do. We want to hear "Well done, good and faithful servant".

This book is dedicated to my late mother, Mary F. Speight. June 21, 1949 - February 8, 2025. She always wanted to write and illustrate a children's book. She is still inspiring me to dream big and to try everything God has put in my heart to do. She was faithfully married to my dad for 52 years and before she feel ill, helped to guide me to live the life I could not even imagine. I love you Mommy, I miss your wisdom about marriage, life and being a godly woman. God is still using a little hardheaded girl from Baltimore like me.

Love your 'lil Mohawk'